KANNUR

KANNUR

INSIDE INDIA'S BLOODIEST REVENGE POLITICS

ULLEKH N.P.

PENGUIN
VIKING
An imprint of Penguin Random House

VIKING

USA | Canada | UK | Ireland | Australia
New Zealand | India | South Africa | China | Singapore

Viking is part of the Penguin Random House group of companies
whose addresses can be found at global.penguinrandomhouse.com

Published by Penguin Random House India Pvt. Ltd
4th Floor, Capital Tower 1, MG Road,
Gurugram 122 002, Haryana, India

First published in Viking by Penguin Random House India 2018

Copyright © Ullekh N.P. 2018
Foreword copyright © Sumantra Bose 2018

10 9 8 7 6 5 4 3 2

The views and opinions expressed in this book are the author's own and the facts
are as reported by him which have been verified to the extent possible, and the
publishers are not in any way liable for the same.

ISBN 9780670090693

Typeset in Adobe Garamond Pro by Manipal Digital Systems, Manipal
Printed at Replika Press Pvt. Ltd, India

www.penguin.co.in

To my father, the late Pattiam Gopalan, for being the voice of reason

Contents

Foreword

I read this book with fascination.

Ever since I became interested in Indian politics as a schoolboy in Calcutta during the 1980s, I have known about the little patch of India called Kannur. It was already notorious for political killings, and the reputation has only grown since.

Last year, I was browsing the in-flight magazine on a domestic flight. As I flipped through the pages, gorgeous photographs of a seaside destination caught my attention. It was a feature on Kannur, which the airline was promoting as a 'hidden gem' of the south. The article was so attractively presented that it made me want to visit there. The only drawback seemed to be that the place is a rather long drive from the nearest airport the airline flies to. That lack of air connectivity is set to end as Kannur's own airport is due to open in 2018.

As a native and a resident of West Bengal, I can relate to the phenomenon euphemistically referred to as 'political violence'. The politics of murder was pioneered in my state by Naxalite militants, who, during their 1969–72 insurrection, vigorously practised the *khatam* (liquidation) line preached by their leaders. The victims included traffic cops, numerous grass-roots activists of the Communist Party of India (Marxist), or the CPI(M), from which the Naxalite stream broke away in 1969, and sundry civilians labelled as enemies of the revolution. The murder of political opponents was normal, almost routine, during the thirty-four years (1977–2011) the CPI(M)-led Left Front ruled West Bengal. In a chapter on state politics in West Bengal in a book on India's contemporary democracy I published in 2013, I noted that the 'intensely adversarial and combative character' of the state's politics 'bred a culture of political violence through the decades of LF rule—including frequent murders of individuals and sporadic small-scale massacres—perpetrated by both camps but especially the ruling CPM'. Most perpetrators, and victims, owed allegiance to the CPI(M) or to the main opposition, the Congress (largely replaced from 1998 onwards by the Trinamool Congress). But in some locales, the CPI(M) engaged in murderous conflict even with the smaller constituent parties of the Left Front. These were turf wars, struggles for local dominance gone toxic—and lethal. The fighting took place between whichever parties were the major players in electoral politics locally. An interesting feature of the Kannur violence is that one of the two main protagonists is the Rashtriya Swayamsevak Sangh (RSS), although the Bharatiya Janata Party (BJP) is no more than a bit player in the region's electoral politics. But as in Kannur, those who have died in West Bengal over the decades have mostly been the 'small fry', people used simultaneously as foot soldiers and cannon fodder.

The incidence of political killings declined sharply after the regime change in West Bengal in mid-2011. But of late, the scourge has returned with a vengeance, under the entrenched rule of the new hegemon of the state's blighted politics.

Ullekh N.P. is uniquely placed to write this chronicle of Kannur, both as a native of the place and as the son of the late Marxist leader Pattiam Gopalan. Being an 'insider'— and a politically connected insider at that—can however pose disadvantages as well as advantages for the writer. It is to Ullekh's credit that he has managed to avoid the pitfalls of being an insider with deep connections to the politics of Kerala and of Kannur. His account is admirably unbiased and impartial. He also writes with an ideal mixture of empathy and detachment. One of the risks of writing about brutality is that the story as told can easily descend into voyeurism, and become a sort of pornography of violence. And this book's subject is as brutal as they come—a true tale of scores, if not hundreds, of macabre, almost ritual-style murders in which those attacked are targeted with swords, surgical knives and other sharp-bladed weapons of local provenance. Ullekh tells the story of unending horror with deadpan factuality, tinged with compassion. In the process, he avoids two temptations that could easily have marred this book: gratuitous sensationalism and excessive sentimentality. At the same time, he fully exploits his profound, native-born knowledge of the history, culture, society and politics of Kannur—and beyond that of Malabar and the rest of Kerala—to produce a finely textured, illuminating narrative.

A week before I sat down to write this foreword in May 2018, a CPI(M) activist and an RSS worker were killed in Kannur—both were stabbed and hacked with sharp weapons, in grisly signature style—within half an hour of each other in Mahé, the one-time French enclave located between Thalassery in Kannur district and Vadakara in Kozhikode district. These were the latest of thirteen political killings in the Kannur area since mid-2016, despite hundreds of peace meetings during the same period at local and district levels, and two high-level meetings held in Thiruvananthapuram and Kannur chaired by Kerala's chief minister. A few days after the twin murders, the chief minister—a native of Kannur who is referred to as 'Modi in a dhoti' by some of his critics—visited the home of the slain CPI(M) cadre to pay his condolences to the family, but not the nearby home of the RSS worker.

The human tragedy of Kannur, etched on the faces of the hundreds of widows and orphans from the blood feuds, represents a deformity and a pathology of Indian politics. The politics of murder is in fact the murder of politics as it *should* be practised in the democracy of a civilized country. We cannot take pride in the maturity of our democracy until this scourge is eradicated, in Kannur and everywhere else.

Kolkata
May 2018

Sumantra Bose
Professor of international and
comparative politics, London School of
Economics and Political Science

1

Waves of Violence

The year 1972. Two weeks after her monsoon wedding, and less than ten months before my twin and I were born, my mother woke up in the wee hours to her brother-in-law's shouts ringing through the house: 'Gopaletta! Someone killed Azhikodan! Comrade Azhikodan is dead!' My father, Pattiam Gopalan, a senior political leader of Kerala and a former member of Parliament, rushed out to fetch the body from Thrissur, along with his colleague M.V. Raghavan. As the men dashed off silently into the dark, the young bride sat in her new home, frozen in shock and fear.

Yet another night in the life of yet another communist wife.

Kannur in North Kerala is home to pristine beaches, among them Asia's largest drive-in beach in the tough-to-pronounce Muzhappilangad. Many decades ago, tourists had not yet set foot here in hordes and it was a hideaway of sorts for young couples who often took a short walk through the sea at low tide to the *thuruth* (island) less than a mile away. It was a place that afforded privacy for lovers.

These days, the beach is crowded with people and vehicles, and the only remnant of those days is a mighty sickle and hammer on the black rocks, erected in concrete, painted scarlet, and now fading in the sunset. Young lovers are still there, bolder and reluctant to leave even at dusk, as though they are waiting for the state-of-the-art footbridge proposed by the government to come up.

Motifs that announce political loyalties adorn not just telephone and electricity posts on the highways of Kerala; even the beachfronts are reflective of an excessively politicized society. Ten kilometres away, the beaches in Azhikode and Kuruva tell the same story. In Payyambalam, close to Kannur's main city centre, the Arabian Sea appears far more turbulent, and strong sea winds force women in saris and skirts to cling to their clothes as they struggle back to the safety of their vehicles, and husbands and brothers turn chivalrous minders ready to chaperone them home or to a movie or to eat out in one of the trendy restaurants that have cropped up in the city. Despite huge remittances from the Gulf, Kannur has made snail-like progress from a hamlet once known mainly for textile exports to a city where an airport is expected to come up shortly.

A hotelier friend says the time isn't yet ripe to launch a five-star hotel here. Ironically, Kannur—a part of Malabar, and once belonging to the princely state of Travancore, which is now in southern Kerala—is the home town of the late patriarch of the Leela Group, Captain Krishnan Nair. The luxury hospitality chain owns prized properties here, but not a hotel.

Along the beach in Payyambalam—which I remember from its less crowded days in the late 1970s—are a crematorium and a graveyard filled with columns and tombs. It is an expansive compilation of the departed who's who of the town. The graves on the left when you approach from the crematorium (it has yet to be electrified) are those of the leftist men and fellow travellers while those on the right are those of leaders and workers of the Congress, the Rashtriya Swayamsevak Sangh and the Bharatiya Janata Party .

Among the prominent names from the Left are the Marxist icon A.K. Gopalan, Swadeshabhimani Ramakrishnapillai (writer and journalist who had been exiled to Kannur) and former chief minister E.K. Nayanar. Some of them are martyrs. Those from the Communist Party of India (CPI) and the Communist Party of India (Marxist), or the CPI(M), which is the biggest communist party in the country, are referred to as *rakthasakshikal* (loosely translated as 'those who had witnessed blood'). The RSS and the BJP call theirs *balidanikal* ('those who sacrificed themselves').

Azhikodan Raghavan was a prominent CPI(M) leader who was on a visit to Thrissur, a district in the former Kochi province, when he was brutally stabbed to death by assailants on the night of 23 September 1972. At the time of his death, he was the state-level convener of the Left Front in Kerala. The column in his name in Payyambalam beach is one of the oldest memorials in the vicinity. Azhikodan was born in the rather downmarket Thekki Bazaar of Kannur town in 1919 and had risen rapidly inside the undivided communist party before he became a stalwart of the CPI(M). Mystery still shrouds his death and nobody has been able to establish any conspiracy behind it though rumours linking Naxalites and Congress leaders, including the late chief minister K. Karunakaran,[1] to his assassination still do the rounds.

The CPI(M) has often alleged that the Congress, then the ruling party, had hired extremist elements to hack Azhikodan to death because they feared that he had proof of corruption by people in high positions in that government, ironically, led by a CPI chief minister, C. Achutha Menon, and remote-controlled by the then home minister K. Karunakaran. The CPI, back then, was seen as a right-wing communist party after the split in 1964 which saw the formation of the CPI(M).[2]

From Thrissur, my father and M.V. Raghavan—both top-level CPI(M) leaders—brought Azhikodan's body to his two-room rented house in Kannur a day after his death and then cremated him at Payyambalam. The police had taken away the papers in his handbag, which he had held tight between his thighs when he lay dying and profusely bleeding from the deep knife wounds; at the scene were a handful of mute spectators and a policeman. Azhikodan had left behind his ninety-year-old mother, wife and five children.

The number of graves in Payyambalam has grown at an alarmingly fast clip since that distant night in 1972, not only because of death by natural causes, but largely due to the murderous politics that some parts of Kannur are known for. Lately, clashes between the RSS and the CPI(M), which had long been confined to certain limited pockets of the district, especially Thalassery and Panoor, have spread to other areas as well, including places such as Payyanur, an otherwise peaceful town.

For decades, the district was known for clashes[3] between the CPI(M) and the Congress; the latter once had a vice-like grip over the region and had persecuted communists with the help of the police. Former top cop Alexander Jacob had compared the relationship between the Congress and the communists in the early decades of independence to that between the British police and the Congress in the pre-independence era. But slowly, the communists began to have the upper hand and their act of using violence as a form of resistance was soon a thing of the past. Yet, stray acts of violence by both these parties persisted, and peaked in the 1990s before the Congress, seemingly accepting the superiority of the Marxists' muscle power, backed down.

One of the most high-profile political assassinations before Azhikodan's that rocked Malabar took place in 1948 when goons with alleged allegiance to the Congress and the police battered to death a former Congress leader, Moyarath Sankaran, who had joined the communist ranks.[4] Born in an aristocratic family in Thalassery, Sankaran was sent to Kolkata to study medicine. While there, he became attracted to the Indian national movement and plunged into Congress activities. Soon, he returned to Malabar to work in the Congress, and took part in various struggles called by Mahatma Gandhi. A brilliant orator and writer, he penned a history of the Congress in the state.

Later, he switched his affiliations to the communist party and took part in peasant movements that had begun to buffet northern Kerala under the leadership of the late communist patriarch and freedom fighter P. Krishna Pillai. About Sankaran's death, E.M.S. Namboodiripad—who was elected Kerala's first chief minister in 1957, a year after the state was formed—wrote: 'A man who used all his potential for the Congress movement in Kerala from its initial days, and nourished it, gets killed by the moral police of that same party . . . what a cruel paradox.'[5] Despite his hectic political work, Moyarath had also devoted time to writing biographies of the likes of C.R. Das and Lala Lajpat Rai, edited letters by Vivekananda, and even started a newspaper. He also helped set up reading rooms and libraries in Kannur.

In the same year, 1948, goons mercilessly beat up communist activist P.C. Ananthan and pushed him to a watery grave in the Kambil River. Similar was the fate of his comrades such as Punnakkodan Kunhambu, V. Narayanan Nambiar and O.P. Ananthan. who were battered to death.

Congress volunteers who espoused non-violence and suffered extreme violence under the British rule were often accused of finding no difficulty in sliding into the skin of the colonialists once India became free.[6] The communists, led by the indomitable P. Krishna Pillai and others, had launched militant peasant movements in the early 1940s, especially in the erstwhile Kannur district, which then had the present-day district of Kasaragod (bordering Karnataka) too in its fold. However, for a couple of decades after freedom from the British, they didn't have the organizational and political wherewithal to resist the onslaught by the ruling classes. The peasant movements that would shape the political culture of Kannur and its adjoining areas began in response to the agrarian crises accompanied by a massive shortage of foodgrain (these will be discussed in the upcoming chapters).

The repressive tactics also invoked a deep craving among the comrades for avenging the humiliations, torture and murders; but they felt helpless in the face of the brute power of the new ruling class of so-called Gandhians and a police force that had been trained by the British.

In the early years of Indian independence, the fear of communism in Asia would force governments, both outside and in India, both at the Centre and in some states, to come down heavily on the communists. The 1948 Calcutta Thesis of the then CPI general secretary B.T. Ranadive[7]—who called for an armed rebellion against the state, much to the anguish of many of his compatriots—would be used to the hilt by the central government to clamp down on the activities of communists across the country. In Kannur, hostilities between the pro-landlord Congress, armed with state power, and the pro-peasant CPI, armed with sticks, were heightened during this period following a ban on the undivided communist party for waging a war against the state.

Allegedly, some Congress functionaries took interest in the official manhunt for communist leaders and volunteers. Unlike in southern Kerala where caste-based movements churned the social fabric of the region, in Malabar and, especially in Kannur, social change triggered primarily by peasant uprisings would result in a deep wedge along political lines. In the south, wherever the caste organizations held sway, there was often a symbiotic relationship between caste groups and political parties. In places like Kannur, such ties were almost non-existent or marginal. Political affiliation therefore became the new identity in Malabar, and marginalized sections found what they had been seeking for long: social identity and political empowerment, thanks to the communist party.

This is not to say that such a relationship between a party member or a sympathizer with the party didn't exist in other parts of Kerala. But the link between the party and the individual was tempered and influenced by the strong presence of caste-based entities in the southern and central parts of the state (all these areas became one unified state, Kerala, on a linguistic basis in 1956). In northern Malabar, so vitiated were political interactions between the Congress and the CPI that even matrimonial alliances were preferred from families belonging to the same party. Party affiliations would become inseparable from familial choices for a long time.

It is not without reason. Until the 1960s, Congress workers far outnumbered the communists who often faced relentless physical assaults and were denied freedom to go about doing party work. In Kannur town, then a stronghold of the Congress, one of the very few communists who successfully organized public meetings and launched into tirades was the legendary leader K.P.R. Gopalan (KPR), who is still recalled with awe by several workers who were part of Balasangham, the then teenage wing of the party.

Dr N.K. Purushothaman, one among them, remembers that before KPR began any speech, he made sure some trained volunteers were assembled in strategic positions at the venue to ward off any ambush, which was routine back in those days.

A section of enlightened Congress leaders of the time such as Sukumar Azhikode and Pamban Madhavan voiced their dissidence and defended democratic values. In fact, citing Azhikode's book *Guruvinte Dukham* (The Guru's Grief), eminent poet K. Satchidanandan brought to light Azhikode's displeasure with the disappearance of values from the Malayali psyche.[8]

Growing up in the late 1970s in Kannur, I remember one of my aunts, a card-carrying member of the CPI(M), warning me from playing football with a boy who was a close relative. She asked me to 'keep a distance' from him and his family because they had tried to spy on us and other relatives during the Emergency. When I stood dazed, she simplified what she meant, 'They are Congress.'

The expression stuck, 'They are Congress.'

The news that hits headlines from Kannur these days is mostly about its law-and-order situation. TV scrolls announce items such as these with great frequency: 'One killed in Muslim League–CPI(M) clashes'; 'Two hurt in RSS–CPI(M) fracas';

'CPI(M) man killed, RSS men nabbed'; 'RSS youth hacked, 7 CPI(M) men held'; 'PFI [Popular Front of India] activists attacked'; 'District Collector calls all-party peace meeting', and so on. The crime bureau statistics, as of November 2016, show that forty-five CPI(M) activists, forty-four BJP–RSS workers, fifteen Congressmen and four Muslim League followers have been killed since 1991 in Kannur, besides a few other murders of the cadres of parties such as the PFI. Between November 2000 and 2016, the number of party workers killed in Kannur was thirty-one from the RSS and BJP, and thirty from the CPI(M), according to data obtained from the police by the independent news website 101reporters.com through a right-to-information request.[9] While the RSS leaders claim that the CPI(M) are now doing to them what the Congress had done to the communists in the past, the CPI(M) leaders contest it, reeling off stats, and claiming that they have been forced to resist because the Hindu nationalists are hoping to effect a religious polarization through the politics of violence in order to reap electoral gains that have eluded them for long.[10]

The latest numbers do not endorse the RSS's claims of being a victim in this Left stronghold. Regardless, the Sangh has actively pursued a campaign, spiffily titled Redtrocity (short for Red Atrocity, referring to the reported high-handedness by the Marxists), as a counterweight to the series of accusations hurled against it for allegedly sowing religious hatred, perpetuating violence against non-conformists, triggering riots and deliberately aiding a mission to heighten communal hostilities. Police records show that the RSS and the BJP have been at loggerheads not with the CPI(M) alone, but also with other parties, including the PFI and the Congress. Yet, equally laughable is the contention by the CPI(M) that it is portrayed as a villain without reason because it has only been engaging in acts of resistance and seldom in violent aggression.

Recent data show that from 1972 to December 2017, of the 200 who died in political violence in Kannur district—which accounted for the highest number of political crimes in the state during the period, far ahead of other districts—seventy-eight were from the CPI(M), sixty-eight from the RSS–BJP, thirty-six from the Congress, eight from the Indian Union Muslim League (IUML), two each from the CPI and the National Development Front (now called the PFI), while the rest were from other parties. Notably, of the total 193 political murder cases that took place in Kannur during the period, 112 of the accused were from the Sangh Parivar and 110 from the CPI(M).[11]

The RSS–BJP argue that the escalation of hostilities started with the killing of an RSS worker on 28 April 1969, but the Marxists aver that the death was a denouement to a series of clashes stemming from the RSS's support to a beedi baron who refused his workers a justified hike in salary and shut his business before floating two new companies.[12] Media reports often show that more communist workers have died in Kannur than those belonging to any other party.[13] The greatest irony in the RSS–CPI(M) fights is that the pro-Hindu Sangh Parivar has had no qualms about targeting CPI(M)-dependent Hindus, while the Marxists, the much-touted saviours of the proletariat, vehemently, so the story goes, go after the working classes who happen to be aligned with the Hindu nationalists.

Along Payyambalam beach, not far from the grave of K.G. Marar, one of the RSS's topmost leaders in the state, is a grave of a twenty-one-year old man. Too young to die, that's what visitors to the place would say. Sachin Gopalan died from sword injuries in July 2012. Allegedly, he was hacked by members of the radical Islamist Campus Front, a feeder organization of the PFI against which the National Investigation Agency (NIA)[14] has now sought a ban for its anti-India activities. Gopal died at a hospital in Mangalore where he had arrived after shifting from one hospital to another in Kannur for want of better facilities. A student of a technical institute in the district, he was attacked when he had gone to a school for political work.

In the darkness of a late windswept evening, standing alone in the forbidding graveyard at Payyambalam, one is filled with evocative visions from the region's chequered past and a violent present caught in the vortex of vendetta politics. When I studied in a boarding school in Thiruvananthapuram, my classmates looked down on my home town as Kerala's Naples, a thuggish backwater; but then the district had contributed two chief ministers (and one more later) as well as several luminaries to the state's cultural, social, professional and political spheres.

I also came to be known as someone from the 'Bihar of Kerala'. Later, I invented a rather self-deprecating phrase of my own: 'the Sicily of Kerala', factoring in the local omertà-like code the Italian region was once known for. Poking fun at oneself does make sense, as it's an effort to tide over the mental fatigue that sets in on being judged as a violent people, who are puritanical and foolish. Deep within, however, it hurts like migraine.

The waves keep breaking hard on the shore like smooth knives on raw flesh.

2

First Blood

Vadikkal Ramakrishnan[1] died in a Thalassery hospital on 28 April 1969 after he was reportedly assaulted by CPI(M) workers. Pinarayi Vijayan, who was elected chief minister of Kerala in 2016, was one of the accused in the case of the murder of the RSS–Bharatiya Jana Sangh (BJS) volunteer who had been a tailor and maker of sweets. In a complaint submitted to the police by a pro-RSS individual, Vijayan says, his name appears first on the list of the accused in the case and lately, the RSS has used social media to play up his alleged involvement in the death of its so-called 'first martyr' in the state. Though the case was dismissed in court, the call to reinvestigate has become shriller, especially after Vijayan became the twelfth chief minister of Kerala.

News reports from the time suggest that Ramakrishnan was killed after he sustained injuries in a counter-attack on the RSS by the CPI(M)—this was in response to the roughing up of a communist student leader, Kodiyeri Balakrishnan, who was returning from the Kodiyeri Junior Basic School & Onion High School in the town. Balakrishnan, who was named the state chief of the CPI(M) in 2015, was sixteen at the time and was beaten up while he was passing by Mukund Talkies, a cinema that stood in a locality called Chettipeedika. His CPI(M) friends struck back in no time, pouncing on Ramakrishnan and others with an axe that they managed to pick up from the brick workers around there. Ramakrishnan had married only a few months earlier.

Another story that did the rounds was that it was not an axe that killed Ramakrishnan, but a crude and yet innovative tool made from the femur of a buffalo; this bone was filled with molten lead, and allowed to cool for days to make it rigid and strong. It would then be covered and tied with cloth.

The report that appeared in the Malayalam daily *Mathrubhumi* the day after Ramakrishnan died (29 April 1969) talks about Kodiyeri Balakrishnan and Ramakrishnan, along with another person, being admitted in the government hospital in Thalassery after inter-party clashes. While Balakrishnan was identified as a member of a CPI(M) feeder organization—the Kerala Students' Federation (KSF), which, in 1970, merged with other state units of the CPI(M) to form the Students' Federation of India (SFI)—Ramakrishnan was named as a member of the Jana Sangh. The report mentions that an axe used by stone workers was used in the attack. It also states that the crime didn't appear to be a premeditated one.

The narrative, however, has changed over time.

Janam TV, a right-wing, pro-Hindutva, nationalist Malayalam channel,[2] aired a report on 13 October 2016, quoting two supposed witnesses, Umesh and Balakrishnan. One of them claimed he was playing marbles and was alerted by war cries from a mob wielding pickaxes and sticks. He alleged he saw Ramakrishnan, with his liver and perhaps other internal organs hanging out, being taken away in an autorickshaw belonging to a person named Johny. The other 'witness' said he saw Pinarayi Vijayan among the group that attacked Ramakrishnan with a pickaxe. Though one of them was a teenager at the time and could not confirm the identity of the assailants, the other did not clearly state that it was Pinarayi Vijayan who attacked Ramakrishnan. But the Janam TV reporter went on to announce that it was Pinarayi Vijayan who killed Ramakrishnan. He concluded that the case was 'sabotaged' at the time, leaving us to interpret that the CPI(M)-led government of E.M.S. Namboodiripad (EMS) had manipulated witnesses to save Vijayan, who was then twenty-three and a youth-wing leader of the CPI(M). The story went viral after PGurus news website picked it up a few days later.[3]

Though the RSS and the BJP[4] don't tire of linking the Kerala chief minister's name to this murder, they are yet to file a petition to reopen the case. In fact, contrary to nationwide claims made by the RSS, Vadikkal Ramakrishnan was not the first victim of Sangh–Marxist clashes in Kerala. That unenviable spot goes to P.P. Sulaiman of Kozhikode. An employee of Gwalior Rayons (now called Grasim) in Mavoor, Kozhikode, he was hacked to death by RSS workers on his way back home from work on 29 April 1968, a year before Ramakrishnan's death. Gwalior Rayons had set up a factory at Mavoor in Kozhikode in the 1960s to produce pulp and fibre. Sulaiman was a vibrant leader of the Left union in the factory and a local CPI(M) leader, according to Kozhikode's district crime records bureau.

Interestingly, the chorus on Vijayan's alleged role in the Ramakrishnan murder case has created confusion among the party ranks, some of whom believe that their leader had a ferocious past. Contemporaries remember Vijayan as an agile, impulsive young man with a propensity for intemperance. Vijayan himself had talked about his impulsive ways in various interviews. His former colleagues such as I.V. Shivaraman, a long-time secretary of the Madayi area committee of the CPI(M) who was Vijayan's senior in the youth federation, and Pattiam Rajan, his college mate at Brennen College in Thalassery— who had worked closely with him in the student and youth arms of the CPI(M) and was nominated to the Kannur district committee and later to the state committee of the party, along with Vijayan—recall the young cadre's hardiness and nerve. In the turbulent days of conflicts among the CPI(M)'s student wing, the SFI, the Congress's Kerala Students' Union (KSU), the RSS's Akhil Bharatiya Vidyarthi Parishad (ABVP), and so on, Vijayan used to train select SFI members in self-defence techniques on campuses in full public view.[5] Vijayan himself had attended the so-called state-level SD (self-defence) camp organized by the CPI(M) in Mananthavady in nearby Wayanad district in the late 1960s.

Vijayan looked up to my father during his early years in politics, and the two remained close friends and comrades till my father's premature death at the age of forty-one in 1978 due to cardiac arrest. In media interviews many years later, Vijayan said time and again that, despite being strong-willed, he had been utterly devastated by the death of Pattiam Gopalan, and that he always stayed away from making speeches at functions marking his death anniversary for fear of becoming emotional on stage.

Over the decades, as he rose through the ranks to become the state secretary of his party and later Kerala's chief minister, Pinarayi Vijayan would become the symbol of the CPI(M)'s muscular politics much more than any of his predecessors, some of whom were his mentors; this made him the darling of party members and the favourite whipping boy of his rivals and a section of the media. In a party that has roots in an ideology that has worldwide acceptance and which holds that the ends justify the means, violence isn't taboo. While this appears politically incorrect in an ideal world, such a thought has led to crucial revolutions in world history—including the French and Russian revolutions, and many other rebellions across the globe that have triggered course corrections, especially when subjugation of the lower strata by the privileged classes became unbearable. Kerala communists tend to quote their ideological Dalai Lama, Karl Marx, to justify their aggression as a working-class party: 'The [written] history of all hitherto existing society is a history of class struggles. Free man and slave, patrician and plebeian, lord and serf, gild-master and journeyman, in a word, oppressor and oppressed, stood in constant opposition to one another, carried on an uninterrupted, now-hidden, now-open fight, a fight that each time ended, either in a revolutionary reconstitution of society at large, or in the common ruin of the contending classes.'[6] Young communists in study classes held by party leaders were taught to memorize these lines in Malayalam. At one time, my peers and I could quote these lines verbatim in both English and Malayalam.

But, having attained a certain kind of dominance for itself, the communist party in Kerala of the nineties had no business in indulging in violence for its own sake or to bully opponents. The era of resistance was over.

I remember a long chat in 1993 with a senior Kannur leader P. Sasi, who later became the political secretary to the late Marxist stalwart and chief minister E.K. Nayanar (between 1996 and 2001). Sasi[7] admitted to me that the party often did 'things' to 'safeguard its interests'—he was explaining the official party version of a rebellion within its ranks caused by a man who had been sentenced for a political murder. On his return from jail, the man claimed that he wasn't involved in the crime, which invited summary expulsion from the party. Even as a young adult, I understood immediately what Sasi meant. Several local-level party workers in Sasi's home village, Mavilayi, told me that the former CPI(M) district secretary used to brag about 'dispatching teams' against political rivals. 'Sasi used to speak as if he were the one at the forefront of the action while he was only remote-controlling from the safety of his position and good life,' one of them said, oblivious to the casualness with which he was painting the picture of criminal violence.

As political debate outside of political parties matured and the call for democratic rights became louder among the aspiring young, the failure of the CPI(M) to adapt to new political realities in the age of 24X7 news and deepening social-media penetration was attributed to the faux sensibilities of its leaders who couldn't cope. Notwithstanding the dominance of politicians who believed in using muscle power, a small section of peaceniks within the party argued that by indulging in violence, the Marxists were only helping the RSS, which they feel is flush with funds, and is fairly capable of creating an 'infrastructure of violence-oriented politics' to make gains in the district and the rest of the state.[8]

When he smiles, which he does often these days, Pinarayi Vijayan comes across as the antithesis of all perceptions about him—both within and outside his party—as a Stalinist control freak. Until a few years ago, it was difficult for even the most nimble of photographers or cameramen to capture his smile as he darted away from questions or turned hostile towards the media. Within the party ranks, there was a joke that the mercurial Vijayan would excuse himself and take a toilet break whenever he wanted to smile or laugh.

In a deliberate PR makeover since taking over as chief minister in 2016, he wears a pleasant smile these days. His public admonitions of insistent TV crews still create national headlines and he is irascible on occasion; yet for those who have known the man for long—as my family and I have—he has mellowed down, in an apparent effort to distance himself from the image of the haughty commissar that he once was. Even so, for the RSS, Vijayan is the most hated leader in Kerala,[9] and it has unleashed its relentless countrywide propaganda, called Redtrocity[10] ever since he came to power in 2016; a part of this propaganda is that its workers have been routinely eliminated under his watch (more in Chapter 7).

Vijayan shrugs off this 'propaganda in the North' as mischievous by reeling off the numbers, but concedes that his party has no way of countering this no-holds-barred 'misinformation' blitz at the national level, be it in the national capital Delhi or in Madhya Pradesh, two places where the Sanghis have staged public protests during his visits.[11] *'Enthayalum aa parippu ivide vevilla,'* he says with a smile, employing a Malayalam phrase whose word-by-word translation goes thus: 'That dal won't cook here.'

Seated in his well-furnished office in Cliff House, Thiruvananthapuram, the official residence of the state's chief minister, Vijayan—respectfully referred to by family and friends as 'Pinarayi', which is actually the name of the village he was born in—pauses for a few moments before recounting the time when locals in Thalassery and Koothuparamba, often the most politically volatile parts of his native Kannur district, believed that the cadres of the RSS were trained in gravity-defying martial-arts skills. They could use their *dandh*, the sticks they carry with them, whenever skirmishes broke out between them and his Marxist colleagues in the most unexpected ways to tackle a large group of people.

This reputation was hyped up through word of mouth, and an RSS *pracharak* with a dandh conjured up images of *kalaripayattu* exponents such as Thacholi Othenan and

Aaromal Chekavar, both master fighters described in the Northern Ballads, the oral narratives that talk of the heroics of medieval *kalari* warriors. Vijayan says this was the scenario in the mid and late sixties when political clashes in his home town were mostly between the Congress party and his own CPI(M), the nascent yet flourishing breakaway group from the CPI; in the elections held a year after the split in 1964, the CPI(M) had displayed early signs of the electoral prowess that it would acquire over the next decades, vastly eclipsing the parent organization. The CPI wanted to align with the national bourgeoisie—meaning the Congress—to take on communal forces; the CPI(M)—a name coined by the election commission to settle the dispute over claims by both parties—wanted no alliance with the Congress, which it considered the class enemy that represented the interests of upper castes in Indian society.

In the 1965 elections in Kerala, Vijayan had worked tirelessly for his party's candidates. Though he had been an active volunteer of the party for years, 1965 was the year he was named a full-time member of the CPI(M). Being a card-carrying member of the CPI(M) meant new responsibilities and a vow of ultimate loyalty to the party. Around then, the RSS was hardly a threat. In the elections held to the state assembly that year, no party could muster a majority in the assembly though the CPI(M) emerged as the single largest entity, effectively decimating the CPI across the state; thus,

President's rule was imposed. Vijayan's party had quarrels with the Congress party and the CPI, whom they called '*valathu communistkar*' (right-wing communists).

There was some relief in street battles during this period, mostly due to the consistently inconsistent ideological affinities of one man. P.R. Kurup[12] of the Praja Socialist Party (PSP)—who routinely targeted all other parties for physical attacks[13]—aligned with the Left bloc in 1965 just before the elections, giving the communists a respite from roadside fracases. But the lull was short-lived as the rank opportunist—who had shifted loyalties several times in his career—moved once again to the Congress camp in the late 1960s.

Kurup was based out of an area called Panoor, which falls in the erstwhile Kadathanadu, home to folk tales of Chekavars and other kalari exponents. Chekavars were warriors who trained day and night since childhood, sparring with each other to protect the honour of their local princelings who hired them to settle scores with other chieftains. An *angam* (bout) was announced even for things as frivolous as who would get the right of way on a narrow road or over verbal abuse. According to Kollam-based former senior police officer Alexander Jacob, who has done extensive research into the life and times of the Chekavars, the practice had been prevalent in Kadathanadu and other areas, which now fall in Kannur and Kozhikode districts, for more than a thousand years. The bouts continued until one of the Chekavars, or both, died. Although modern political scientists have ruled out a link between such a blood sport and the ongoing vendetta politics in Kannur, there are studies that argue that the making of the violence today is embedded in its volatile past (more in Chapter 4).

The year 1967 changed Indian politics like never before with the Congress party tasting defeat in some of its strongholds in the first General Elections held after the death of the first prime minister, Jawaharlal Nehru. However, his daughter, Indira Gandhi, cruised to power to head the Congress-led government at the Centre, securing seventy-eight seats fewer compared with the previous General Elections held in 1962. The year also saw a significant growth in right-wing nationalism and provincial chauvinism as a political force. The BJS, the political arm of the RSS and predecessor to the current ruling BJP, made decent gains in the elections to the Lok Sabha, winning thirty-five seats, its highest ever. While the CPI won twenty-three seats and the CPI(M) nineteen, the pro-market Swatantra Party led by former Congress stalwart C. Rajagopalachari—the country's first Indian governor general and a close associate of Mahatma Gandhi and Nehru—polled forty-four.

In Kerala, the Congress fared even worse: it lost all seats except one to the Opposition. And in the state assembly elections held simultaneously, the CPI(M)-led seven-party Saptakakshi Munnani came to power under the leadership of the CPI(M)'s E.M.S. Namboodiripad. The CPI, the Muslim League, the Revolutionary Socialist Party (RSP) and others were initially part of this coalition, but by 1969, they broke ranks and aligned with the Congress, resulting in the fall of the CPI(M)-led ministry.

The year 1967 also marked the emergence of a new opponent in the battlefield for Kannur's Marxists: the RSS. With its political arm, the BJS, having made large gains in the Lok Sabha, the nationalist right-wing organization was rather desperate for regional wins too. Its local Kannur cadre, so far uninspired to take up arms against their communist rivals, found a new confidence to do so.

Considering such rapid political changes in the state, it is fairly easy to deduce that Vadikkal Ramakrishnan's death was certainly a denouement to a series of violent clashes that ensued.

As a young comrade of the CPI(M) battling local Congress elements, Pinarayi Vijayan also wanted to call the RSS's bluff when it bared its fangs, he declares, but that wasn't easy. The fear was palpable among his own partymen who, he says,[14] were routinely terrorized by the RSS workers in various pockets of Thalassery town where the Hindutva outfit had some influence, thanks to a handful of local toughies they had co-opted. The terror tactics that were used also evoked a reluctant admiration for the martial skills of the RSS volunteers.

After the BJS's good performance in north India in 1967 under the presidency of Balraj Madhok, the RSS was excited about its poll prospects. It was around this time that the communists registered a landslide win in Kerala, both in the state and national elections held simultaneously. The government led by EMS also brought in pro-labour reforms in the beedi sector. As academics[15] have pointed out, the beedi workers were a mainstay of the leftist movement in the state, so it was only natural that Kerala decided to implement a central government legislation passed in 1966 related to the beedi–cigar industry. The federal Act had included several provisions to ensure the welfare of the beedi workers. Some of them were:[16]

> No employee shall be required or allowed to work in any industrial premises for more than nine hours on any day or for more than forty-eight hours in any week; provided that any adult employee may be allowed to work in such industrial premises for any period in excess of the limit

fixed under this section subject to the payment of overtime
wages if the period of work, including overtime work, does
not exceed ten hours on any day and in the aggregate fifty-
four hours in any week; where any employee employed in
any industrial premises is required to work overtime, he
shall be entitled in respect of such overtime work, to wages
at the rate of twice his ordinary rate of wages.

The EMS government implemented such provisions in
September 1968, attracting criticism from beedi barons,
especially those in North Malabar. They argued that these
measures to bring beedi workers under the factory laws were
unrealistic, a position shared by the RSS which reportedly
had strong financial links with Mangalore Ganesh Beedi,[17]
which decided to shut shop in Kerala on 15 October 1968.
That meant 12,000 workers lost their jobs. The company
also warned that unless the workers' unions relinquished their
claims, it wouldn't run its operations in the state.

But then the company knew only too well that quality
beedis could be made only by those highly skilled workers
from Kerala. So, its Karnataka-based proprietors, with solid
RSS links, decided to enter Kerala through what began to
be known as '*kangani pani*', a derogatory expression for a
system whereby the company would deliver raw materials
to homes of select workers, but not offer them any place to
work. To keep the new laws at bay, it also managed to hire

as manager a seasoned RSS man, an amiable former Indian railways employee Chandrasekharan, popularly known as Chandrettan. He left his earlier job to take charge of one of the three new companies that Mangalore Ganesh Beedi had floated in the state to beat the new guidelines—Mahalaxmi Traders. The other two were Guru Kripa and Deepak Tobacco. Their depots were opened to collect the beedis rolled by the workers from their homes. Most of those who found employment through the new route were RSS sympathizers—because the very reason why the RSS had cooperated with the Mangalore-based beedi tycoon was to rehabilitate them, says P. Narayanan, a former editor of *Kesari* newspaper and a seasoned RSS leader. According to him, the beedi units had become a nursery of sorts for recruiting members to the CPI(M), and were also routinely hosting party classes. The new system suited the RSS agenda very well.

The Marxists thought this was an anti-worker step by outstation beedi barons to circumvent state rules and float new companies with an eye merely on profit. It infuriated them that the company owners didn't value the highly skilled beedi workers of Kannur, who were the backbone of the industry. Such indifference to the welfare of the workers had to be resisted at all cost, they decided. They also resented that the RSS was working as a private army for Mangalore-based tycoons.

The stage was set for a major conflict.

The CPI(M) leaders began to look for a solution. It occurred to them that a cooperative had to be set up to house the beedi workers who had lost their jobs. The idea of launching Kerala Dinesh Beedi was born. The plan would come to fruition only in 1969, and until then, the beedi workers were on strike. This phase was destined to trigger major confrontation in the district between pro-CPI(M) workers and the RSS, which was unabashedly in favour of Mangalore Ganesh Beedi and its three subsidiaries in the state.

In response to the demand for reopening the shut-down units, the company, through its chief negotiator, argued that 'there had not been any conciliation talks', because, according to him, conciliation talks are held when there is a labour dispute. According to *Mathrubhumi* newspaper (7 November 1968 and 23 November 1968), which reported the incident, the negotiator said that the employee–employer relationship had ceased to exist between the management of Mangalore Ganesh Beedi and its workers. The negotiator wanted all the trade unions (including the RSS-steered Bharatiya Mazdoor Sangh, or BMS) to accept the 'outwork system' where payments were low. He also wanted the state government not to insist on past labour liabilities.

As Thomas Isaac and co-authors[18] point out in their book on Kerala Dinesh Beedi, the employers' demands were a virtual declaration of war against the state government and the beedi unions. Such an outrageous position that sought a free hand to break the law meant confrontations were about to heighten further. The RSS squads had no qualms about offering protection to the managers of Mahalaxmi Traders at its depots in the wake of the strike becoming violent. Their justification was that the state was becoming increasingly anti-business under communist rule.

It was during this time that R. Raghavan, the Thalassery unit secretary of the CPI(M), was reportedly stopped on his way home one late evening and warned to stay off the RSS's path. Various other CPI(M) workers were routinely harassed near Chettipeedika either while they were passing by or when they went to watch movies at Mukund Talkies. In hindsight, Pinarayi Vijayan feels that the RSS sensed an opportunity to browbeat the Left in Kerala over labour issues due to what was happening in India's commercial capital, Bombay (now Mumbai).

During this time, the rise of the provincial Shiv Sena, a right-wing political entity floated in the name of the Maratha hero Chhatrapati Shivaji, had been rapid, catapulting its leader Bal Thackeray to the national limelight. Its postures struck a chord with the locals in Bombay whose frustrations at being unemployed and underemployed were displaced by Thackeray through rabble-rousing and delivering sectarian speeches which pointed at their enemy number one: the southerner. These divisive sentiments whipped up by the Shiv Sena would shortly decimate the communists and the leftist trade unions in the city touted as India's commercial capital.

Author and senior journalist Sujata Anandan uncovered the conspiracies that took place behind the scenes in Bombay. 'By [Bombay-based businessman and architect] Madhav Deshpande's own admission, Congress leaders then sent him bags of cash to take care of meetings that the [Shiv] Sena might hold or to put up candidates against those of the communist parties to cut into their vote bank by raising the regional sentiment against that of workers' unity. That's how they defeated former Union defence minister V.K. Krishna Menon who had contested from Bombay North with communist support after he was denied a ticket by the Congress on account of his role in India's debacle in the 1962 war with China.'[19] Historian Juned M. Shaikh also captured in his essays the outcome of the reported Congress strategy to prop up the Shiv Sena as a counterweight to the communists and the Left trade unions in Mumbai and the rest of Maharashtra. In his article titled 'Worker Politics, Trade Unions and the Shiv Sena's Rise in Central Bombay',[20] he wrote: 'In the mill districts of Central Bombay, there was a keen tussle for political supremacy between the leftist trade unions and a right-wing party called the Shiv Sena. The Shiv Sena's right-wing image can be culled from a few repetitive themes in its mouthpiece, the weekly *Marmik*. Some of these themes were anti-communism, Maharashtrian pride,

Indian nationalism, and Hindu identity.' He analysed how the new entity in the late 1960s made a deep impact among the middle classes and the working-class population of the city. It also won the municipal elections. Shaikh added, 'The Shiv Sena's electoral gains in Central Bombay were at the expense of the Left parties and the Congress. Similarly, the trade union wing of the Shiv Sena made a dent in the support base of the entrenched unions of the Left and the Congress parties in various industries of the city, including the textile mills of central Bombay.'

'That must have been an inspiration to the RSS to take on the Left in Kannur over a trade-union issue,' asserts Vijayan. The RSS, which is intimately linked with Maharashtra politics and its dynamics, apparently felt that drumming up pro-Hindu sentiments in a thickly Muslim-populated region such as Thalassery might help improve its fortunes in Kerala in the long run. Thalassery, home to affluent Muslims and a large chunk of marginalized and impoverished Hindus, was seen as the ideal turf to spark off a religious conflict. Here, there has been a long-standing rivalry between the moneyed classes that goes back several decades.

As the political crisis in Thalassery worsened, with clashes becoming frequent, C.H. Kanaran, the then state secretary of the CPI(M), came visiting. Kanaran, hands-on and assiduous at pointing out tactical faults of the party, said at a party meet that Vijayan should take over as the new unit secretary. 'I said no because I was very young,' Vijayan tells me. But Kanaran was not someone who would take no for an answer. And Vijayan had to relent.

In his new position, Vijayan was determined to fight against the frequent harassment of party cadres. He says RSS leaders led by one Sreedharan and his brothers in the Kolasseri region of Thalassery made life hell for his partymen, especially the hapless beedi workers. 'In Chettipeedika, the situation was much worse,' he says, emphasizing that his name was dragged into the case as part of a conspiracy to target the new leadership. 'In the case involving Ramakrishnan's murder, I wasn't remanded even for an hour in any police station, because the court was absolutely convinced that I was not part of it,' Vijayan avers. And as luck would have it, Ramakrishnan's death would result in immediate cessation of hostilities between the CPI(M) and the RSS.

But that was the calm before the storm.

3

Vignettes of Grief and Rage

The storm has left behind colossal sorrow, and the bitterness is infectious.

Though his wife had raised eyebrows over the length of their names, C.V. Dhanaraj insisted that his sons, eight years apart, be called Vivekananda and Vidyananda. Sajini had heard of Dhanaraj as a known local activist of the CPI(M) years before they actually met. A natural leader with a disarming, jaunty smile, Dhanaraj befriended Sajini after they started working at a cooperative bank in the neighbourhood. By the time the two got married on 30 January 2005, he had shifted to the construction business and all that the young wife looked forward to was upward mobility and a peaceful life.

However, on 11 July 2016, around 9.30 p.m., her dreams were shattered as forty-one-year-old Dhanaraj lay bleeding to death in the shed behind their house. A few minutes earlier, he had dropped off a companion who was riding pillion on his bike less than a kilometre away. When his bike slowed down to a halt in front of his house, seven assailants wielding machetes struck their deadly blows. Instead of running into the house and endangering his family, he ran behind to the shed—where the family stored household items such as firewood—in a final race to cling on to life under the cover of darkness. But it was too late. His assailants left nothing to chance. The last five minutes of his life ended in a pool of hot blood and warm flesh.

Sajini heard the commotion and rushed out to see a gang vanish; she even managed to grab an attacker's hand as he pulled away. Then she darted forward, hoping not to see what she would soon see. Her momentary hope was that Kunnoru, their village at the foothills of the Ezhimala Naval Academy, had not seen any political violence—and why would her beloved husband be the target of a mercenary attack? Of course, Dhanaraj had received threats for organizing youths in an area not far from a few RSS pockets. (The police say there are 'RSS villages' nearby, such as Kakkampara and Mottakunnu, and antisocial elements there have direct access to killer squads from Mangalore.) Dhanaraj's party had taken the threats seriously and had insisted that he be accompanied by someone—and that someone was with him less than a kilometre from his home.

Sajini and Dhanaraj were not just partners in life but also very good friends. They chatted about their children and friends after supper; that night Sajini had finished preparing dinner and was waiting for her husband. Instead, she ended up waiting for his funeral where her dearest man was draped in a red shawl and taken to the pyre by CPI(M) volunteers dressed in red and khaki uniforms, with a band squad in tow.

Mourning women can get hardened. Dhanaraj's mother, Madhavi, who had begged the killers to spare her son that night, now doesn't care about visitors at home. She ignores everyone—friends, family, strangers. She has withdrawn into herself, having lost her only son, the other two children being daughters who are married and live far away. The local CPI(M) leaders say that the mother is sometimes 'nasty' with strangers, especially scribes. Mothers who lose their sons have their own ways of coping, especially once the grief has disappeared from their faces and gone deeper within.

Sajini, too, isn't pleased about the attention: she knows speaking to journalists will not allay her grief. She has gone back to work at the bank because, eleven years into her marriage, she has two sons to tend for, and wants to see her husband's dream come true: a good education for them. The CPI(M) is currently building a new house for her next to the older one so that the family can start afresh.

Sajini pats her younger son on his head and stares into his face, her motherly devotion and love momentarily eclipsing her worries about them. Behind her, on the discoloured wall, hangs a picture of Dhanaraj in a dusty frame. Unlike typical Marxist households, one cannot immediately spot photos of Lenin, Stalin, Che Guevara and others here. But the sight of a young widow and her grieving mother-in-law seated beneath photos of their beloved dead is sickeningly commonplace.

After a while, Sajini stops answering my questions. 'Nothing can bring my husband back,' she says, dry-eyed.

Within three hours after the assailants, allegedly with links to the RSS, slayed Dhanaraj, whom a police officer describes as a likeable but hard-nosed CPI(M) worker with a bit of aggression about him, a leader of the BMS was murdered in Payyanur in a revenge attack. The modus operandi was along expected lines: hurl country-made bombs and then stab the target to death.[1]

The victim, C.K. Ramachandran, was an autorickshaw driver. That night, he had had dinner with his wife, Rajini, and their teenaged twins, thirteen-year-old Devangana and Devadathan. Upset after seeing the news on TV about Dhanaraj's murder, he had gone to bed. It wasn't long before a bomb went off outside their house and the attackers began to target the main door after going on a rampage of destruction outside, crushing his autorickshaw into pulp with sticks. The couple pushed themselves against the door so that it couldn't be breached. But their efforts proved futile. When the enraged men broke in, Rajini pleaded—she has repeated the claim in TV interviews, including to Manorama TV—with one of them, Nandakumar, whom she knew well, and asked him to leave her man alone. 'Nandan, if you tell them, they won't hurt him,' she implored.

However, none of that helped. Nandan shoved her away and, in the process, her nightdress tore. Then they pounced on Ramachandran, knifed him repeatedly and left him to die before he reached the hospital. Not a single soul came to their aid, for obvious reasons.

Rajini's children had seen it all happen right in front of them. But they still hope their father may return from a long journey, some day.

In another related ritual of murder, almost a year later in May 2017, thirty-five-year-old Choorakkadu Biju, an RSS functionary and the twelfth accused in the murder of Dhanaraj, was chased by a silver Innova and hacked to death. He was riding pillion on a bike and was intercepted and killed on a bridge at Palakkode near Payyanur. As his bike lay whirring, the killers got away, the roar of their Innova fading into the distance. Before Biju's death, the CPI(M) and the RSS had come together to talk peace.

The talks didn't stop more deaths—in Kannur, there is a euphemism for such revenge killings: goal scoring.

Violence between RSS and CPI(M) workers used to be fairly unusual in Payyanur. Things are different, though, in Valankichal near Koothuparamba, which has witnessed occasional fights involving CPI(M) and RSS workers. Yet, not even Sangh workers expected fifty-two-year-old K. Mohanan to be a target. He was just another friendly local leader of the CPI(M) who ran a toddy shop. Unlike in other neighbouring areas of Koothuparamba and Thalassery, Valankichal had not seen any heightened political hostilities resulting in deaths, which also explains why the amiable Mohanan shared good relations with the local RSS men, many of whom, even those older than him, called him Mohanettan (*ettan* stands for 'older brother') out of respect. He was actually a darling of the people in his neighbourhood, irrespective of party loyalties, and had no criminal record at all. It was Mohanan who helped his struggling neighbour, Ibrahim, build a new home so that he could hold a decent wedding for his daughter.

Yet, Mohanan was killed by alleged RSS workers. This took place on 10 October 2016, around 10 a.m., inside the toddy shop where he had returned after buying chicken. His colleague, too, was stabbed, but he survived. Mohanan's wife, Suchithra, has still not been able to come to terms with the loss. She was married to Mohanan at the age of eighteen and has two grown-up children, twenty-one-year-old Mithun, a promising hockey player who does odd jobs, and twenty-year-old Sneha who, as I write this, is a student.

Seated in the veranda of her home, Suchithra, who works with the Kerala State Rubber Co-operative Limited (Rubco), tells me that she didn't initially believe that her husband was murdered. For a long while, she assumed it was just a rumour—he could never be a victim of political violence. The intense agony of someone's personal loss can never be gauged by others, she adds, bursting into tears continually, and explaining how Mohanan's death has thrown everything out of gear. She appears bone-tired, and the worry lines are visible on her forehead. 'I have never ever taken allopathic medicine before in my life. Now I have to take some five tablets twice every day for high blood pressure and a host of other health complications. I can't sleep and I am worried about my children's future,' she says, her hands shaking. She can't help but wonder why the killers targeted a harmless man like her husband.

Mithun says he is anxious about his mother, who he believes has not recovered from the shock of her husband's death. 'As a young man, I have come to terms with it, but I still wonder why it happened. My father wasn't involved in any violent activities; on the other hand, he had even helped some BJP workers in times of need,' he says. His eyes are grave, and reflect the sparks of anger firmly reined in.

A memorial has been erected—at the spot where Mohanan was cremated—in the compound of their home, but Suchithra has not looked at it even once. 'I don't have the strength to face him.'

The concept of 'number *ittu kollal*' (murder to equal the tally) is not new to Kannur. The late Marxist leader M.V. Raghavan,[2] who in his later years joined the Congress-led coalition in the state after he was expelled from the party, had said in the last years of his life that he completely disapproved of political violence which resembled a mafia-like operation where, if you don't avenge the killing of a gang member, you are immediately treated as a nonentity. For most of his life, Raghavan had been a symbol of Kannur's murderous politics. He left the party in 1986, but many of his former lieutenants who had stayed back in the CPI(M) and rose to leadership positions never bothered to reconsider their rigid and violent ways.

Mohanan knew almost all of the six-member execution squad who had darted into his toddy shop to butcher him, says Ashokan, Mohanan's colleague. Their face masks were not effective enough to hide their identities, he says.

The dead comrade had several plans for his neighbourhood: to set up a yoga centre, to organize sports competitions, rehabilitate stray dogs, and so on.

A pack of strays lingers outside the shop, perhaps waiting for the hand that fed them.

Chodon Uthaman, a BJP worker and a bus driver, who was killed in 2002 by political rivals in a place called Keezhur, had left behind a grieving wife and two children. After her husband's killing, her children were the ones who gave Narayani some sense of purpose in life, and she raised them as best she could. Once they grew up, she married her daughter off, while her son, Remith, went to the Gulf for work. He later returned to Kerala and began working as a taxi driver.

In October 2016, Narayani's pregnant daughter had come home for her delivery. For the first time in a long while, Narayani was happy: her daughter was going to have a child, and pretty soon, they would find her twenty-six-year-old son a bride. Remith—whom his family claims was not linked to any party but whom the BJP claims was a party activist—and his family lived in Pinarayi, the native village of Kerala's chief minister, which is not far from where Mohanan was brutally killed.

A day before Mohanan's murder, the RSS and BJP leaders in and around Remith's village had gone into hiding; very few of them were available even on their cell phones, the police tell me. The CPI(M) men were aching for revenge.

Two days after Mohanan died, Remith stepped out of his home to buy medicines for his pregnant sister. Before he knew it, a band of killers charged at him with swords and knives. They slit his throat, and left a while later after confirming that their prey wouldn't live to tell the tale.

A neighbour tells me with a straight face that it would have been more humane if the attackers had killed the mother too—at least Narayani would have been spared the sorrow of having to live with multiple scars. 'After the father, it is now the son. Imagine the gravity of the tragedy that violence unleashes on families. And this is one family where two lives have been lost from two generations,' he says, emphasizing that though he himself is pro-Left, a young person's death is always a cause of anguish, no matter what their political affiliation may be. 'In a highly educated and politically aware society like Kerala, no such deaths should take place, but what we are witnessing is a spate of such killings.'

Forty-eight hours after the death of a local CPI(M) leader, an alleged BJP activist was murdered, and his ashes merged with his father's at the compound of their home.

On 12 October 2016, BJP president Amit Shah tweeted, 'Attacks on BJP *karyakarta*s in CM Pinarayi Vijayan's home constituency is a matter of grave concern and smacks of political vendetta.'[3]

Very soon after Pinarayi Vijayan was elected chief minister in May 2016, two CPI(M) men were killed—on 19 May, P.V. Raveendran, who was taking part in the CPI(M)'s victory celebrations died in a bomb attack, and on 11 July, C.V. Dhanaraj was killed in Kannur. And then, the game of retaliation started.

The RSS–BJP's Ramachandran[4] was killed in the wee hours of 12 July 2016, and Biju on 5 May 2017, to avenge Dhanaraj's death. On 3 September 2016, twenty-five-year-old RSS activist Mavila Vineesh[5] was hacked to death in Thillenkeri village in Kannur two hours after a bomb was hurled at the CPI(M) youth leader Jijesh who was travelling in a car. On 18 January 2017, Ezhuthan Santhosh,[6] a fifty-two-year-old RSS activist, was done to death by an armed gang that broke into his house at Andaloor in Dharmadam at night.

Several months after the gruesome incident, I visited the new home near Melur where the wife and children of the slain RSS worker Santhosh now live, but they had gone to Andaloor for some work. I then checked with the police to get more details of the attack. They told me that the incident followed minor clashes in the area, which included two stabbings of CPI(M) workers a week earlier. The police said that Santhosh suffered twenty stab wounds. While he was being taken to hospital, he disclosed the names of his attackers.

Over the past two years in Kannur—besides these deaths—there have been several attacks on the lives of political activists of various outfits. Sreejan Babu barely escaped death after battling for life in hospitals for months. When I met him two months after he was attacked on 3 July 2017, he could hardly get up from his bed (his wife helped him up), and there were scars of deep wounds running all over his body. An autorickshaw driver and CPI(M) branch committee member, the forty-three-year-old was attacked while he was inside his vehicle on Nayanar Road at Ponniam in Thalassery. Babu tells me that he saw his attackers coming from different sides, but before he could run, they closed in on him. Though they wore masks, he says he could identify them by their body language and movements. Babu's wife, A.K. Ramya, who is the panchayat president of Eranholi, told me in an interview in September 2017 that when she got a call saying that her husband was unwell, she was in no hurry to leave her office—since he had not been involved in any cases earlier, she had no reason to worry about him. Babu interjects to say that his attackers were young men whom he describes as 'antisocial', who forcibly collected money from neighbours and harassed women. 'They had no political affiliations initially, but the RSS, which does not have as much influence in the panchayat, decided to co-opt them so that they could be used for their . . . tricks,' declares the father of an eleven-year-old boy. Babu was attacked hours before the district-level peace talks were to take place in Kannur. Several months after the attack, Babu hasn't recovered and lives in his wife's home next to verdant fields. The former footballer regrets that he can't walk around without help.

The Thalassery MLA A.N. Shamseer argues that, of late, supposed 'RSS goons' have been adopting a new approach of maiming victims so badly that they can never live normally for the rest of their lives. Besides Sreejan Babu, he mentions the names of three 'mere CPI(M) sympathizers' who were mercilessly assaulted by RSS cadres recently: forty-seven-year-old Dr K.T. Sudheer Kumar, who is the son of K.C. Chandran, a former municipal chairman of Mattanur, and thirty-eight-year-old Sreejith, who was targeted near the Ayyallur library in Mattanur, along with Sudheer on the night of 25 December 2017. They did not lose their lives, but doctors have stated that they would find it tough to get back to work.

What Shamseer doesn't disclose, though, is that the area was tense following the attacks on five RSS and CPI(M) men in the preceding months.

In the month of October 2017, an RSS activist, Nidhish, was knifed by a group of people. Similar were the fates of a CPI(M) worker, K.P. Sharath, and an RSS functionary, Sujeesh, who were seriously injured in separate attempts on their lives on the night of 13 November 2017, near Panoor, a nerve centre of clashes between political opponents.

Politicians often make wild claims about the deaths of their rivals. While an RSS leader tells me that Raveendran of the CPI(M) had died after being run over by a car carrying party revellers after the assembly poll victory, the CPI(M) state secretary Kodiyeri Balakrishnan says that Santhosh of Andaloor was killed following a land dispute. It's another story that some senior district-level CPI(M) leaders paid a visit to the RSS activist's family after his death in a novel gesture suggested by the district administration in order to offer an olive branch. They met Santhosh's wife and daughter, who were taken aback to see Marxist leaders at their home. It was an unprecedented move.

Party leaders also hasten to tell the grieving mothers, sisters, wives, brothers, sons and daughters that they are not alone, and that the party is with them in their collective grief.

But one can never be sure. In Kannur's spiral of political violence, the perpetrators are indistinguishable from the victims amid the propaganda war between the warring political entities bent on 'levelling scores', as a party leader of the RSS tells me. Last year, bombs went off at the home of Valayangadan Raghu, an RSS worker in Koothuparamba; similar news items about Marxist workers getting wounded from explosions apparently caused while storing country bombs are not rare. Self-defence camps and arms training are routine for both camps.

Between August 1987 and August 2017, the number of BJP–RSS activists murdered stood at forty-seven, CPI(M) at forty-six, and others at twenty-seven.

Amidst all this turmoil, the mourners are inconsolably lonely.

I remember P. Jayarajan from the time I started remembering faces. Back then, he had a pencil-thin frame. My uncles tell me he was even thinner earlier. He had always had a friendly demeanour about him; so much so that, it is said, during the Emergency, he was not considered by the police to be 'an SFI type' and therefore could be put to use as a 'courier', who could carry messages between the party leaders and workers.

Jayarajan's name resurfaced in my scheme of things when M.V. Raghavan was first suspended and then dismissed from the party in 1986. Jayarajan was known to be close to MVR—as the leader was known among his adoring cadres—and had come into prominence as a close ally of Pattiam Rajan, a former MP and CPI(M) state committee member, who later joined MVR's party after the split in 1986. A senior leader is said to have approached Jayarajan to invite him to join the new party. However, Jayarajan, despite all his hero worshipping of MVR, decided not to leave the CPI(M). Unlike many others, he didn't wait till it was abundantly clear as to who would gather more forces, either MVR or the official leadership. At a time when people still believed in the Soviet dream—after all, the Soviet Union had not crumbled yet—it didn't take long for anyone to know which side would have the last laugh, especially with E.M.S. Namboodiripad making shrewd, public moves to paint Raghavan as a villain so that the latter would retaliate, and then the party could use the plank of 'indiscipline' to show him the door.

After MVR's departure, Jayarajan stood firm, and made a name as a firebrand who often visited RSS strongholds in his area and made provocative speeches. Cadres seemed to be in awe of him for his brave posturing, a style he may have picked up from MVR, his political mentor. As a leader who roughed it out in the grime and dust of the turbulent politics of the time—in Koothuparamba and nearby areas, the party was faced with attacks from multiple quarters—he expected some political gains to come his way. He had been rewarded with organizational posts, much coveted in a communist party. When the 1987 elections came around, former chief minister E.K. Nayanar was expected to be fielded from the Koothuparamba assembly seat, but at the last minute he was shifted to a safer Thrikkaripur seat after the sitting MLA, O. Bharathan, was moved to the Edakkad constituency.

This meant Jayarajan stood a chance to contest the polls from Koothuparamba, and he lost no time in openly stating that he was going to be the candidate, an act, back then, which would be deemed 'anti-party' and unexpected of a communist. But the party leadership, especially Pinarayi Vijayan, who had disapproved of Jayarajan's links with MVR, had other plans. A rather unknown K.P. Mammu Master was fielded as the CPI(M) candidate from Koothuparamba at the last minute. Jayarajan took this as a personal affront and offered to resign his organizational position as the secretary of the Koothuparamba area committee. Though a team of party leaders, including Vijayan, and O. Bharathan, managed to convince Jayarajan to lie low, the blot lingered. 'How can a party leader crave candidacy and act whimsically?' 'Wasn't this an act of deviation, which reeked of greed for parliamentary positions?' Such were the remarks the comrades made in those days. Jayarajan had to wait fourteen more years, till 2001, to become an MLA.

The most defining political moment in Jayarajan's[7] life came on the day of Onam, the Malayali festival of harvest, in 1999. 'I used this one to eat rice until I was forty-nine,' he tells me, pointing at his right hand. The story is now part of communist lore in the district: on the day of Onam, a murderous assault on Jayarajan was carried out, allegedly, by RSS activists. He suffered severe wounds on his spinal cord, limbs and chest, and nearly died.[8]

Jayarajan had been resting at his then home in Kizhakke Kathiroor after the Onam feast when his wife Yamuna woke him up from his rare siesta. She was serving him tea when, suddenly, explosions rocked the floor and rattled the windows. A neighbour, Kanaka, ran towards Jayarajan's home, screaming. More bombs went off and, as Jayarajan narrated to me in three interviews in 2014, 2015 and 2017, he allegedly saw RSS people, many of them familiar faces, barge in with axes, machetes and cleavers. They pushed through the main door, which Jayarajan and his wife tried to slam shut in vain, and threw a bomb inside the house before attacking him physically. It proved to be a strategic mistake. Some of them lost all sense of direction amid the billowing smoke in the massive blast.

Jayarajan, on his part, tentatively looked about to see what was happening when he came face-to-face with his assailants. Trained in the martial art of kalaripayattu, he tried to resist by wielding the plastic chairs lying in the room, but it didn't work for obvious reasons and he had to flee to the inner rooms and then to the toilet. He still remembers the 'Om Kali Bhadrakali' shouts before he received the first cuts. The attackers continued exploding bombs as he lay in a puddle of blood, immobilized by the attacks.

Long before Yamuna called up the party office in Koothuparamba and the cadres came with vehicles to ferry him to the Thalassery Cooperative Hospital, he had fallen unconscious. When he regained consciousness, he couldn't open his eyes, which were flooded with blood. The pain from the damage to the spinal cord made him feel that his strength was ebbing away. The complex nature of the wounds meant that he had to be taken for advanced medical care in Kochi, and it was on the way in an ambulance that he disclosed the names of his attackers to fellow comrades who were inside the vehicle. The ambulance made an emergency stop at the Kozhikode Medical College where expert doctors checked his wounds. After finally reaching Kochi's Specialists Hospital, he had to be operated on for the next thirteen hours—any delay in accessing such specialized treatment would have crippled him for life. Even so, there was no chance that he would ever lead a normal life again. The attempt on the life of Jayarajan was followed by state-wide condemnations as well as conjectures. The date 25 August 1999, in hindsight, was destined to shift the CPI(M)'s focus away from the Congress, which had already begun to see its strong-arm politicians distancing themselves from their earlier violent ways (though they continued to fish in troubled waters), to the RSS.

The RSS has officially denied its role in the attack, but when in 2007, six people, including two of its known workers, were sentenced by a lower court to rigorous imprisonment, the organization appealed against the verdict in the Supreme Court and later obtained a stay. These included K. Ajith, C. Prashant, K. Manu, P. Sasidharan, E. Manoj and K. Jayaprakash. Two of these names—E. Manoj and P. Sasidharan—would keep surfacing repeatedly in the narration of Kannur's bloodstained politics. While E. Manoj would meet his end in 2014, Sasidharan, also called 'Para' Sasi (*para* meaning rock), would reportedly continue to hold control over killer squads in the district, evolving himself, allegedly, into a mastermind behind several anti-CPI(M) strikes. He walks around these days flanked by paramilitary guards.[9]

Effectively, a final verdict on the Jayarajan case has yet to be delivered, though the RSS has unofficially confirmed its role behind the attempt on his life. In a speech uploaded on YouTube, RSS leader Valsan Thillenkeri describes how the attack on Jayarajan came about.[10] He paints the CPI(M) leader as a psychopath who had destroyed an RSS worker's home in his Kathiroor neighbourhood and planted a coconut tree where the home stood. Thillenkeri also claims that Jayarajan was targeted for denying the exiled RSS worker Prashanth 'permission' to celebrate Onam at his home in Kathiroor. According to Thillenkeri, Prashanth's father had to go begging to Jayarajan to seek his nod to allow his son to visit his home on the auspicious day. The RSS leader alleges that Jayarajan told Naanu Master, a CPI(M) sympathizer and father of the RSS worker, that his son had to stay away. Similar stories tarnishing Jayarajan have been in circulation lately after the Central Bureau of Investigation (CBI) took up the E. Manoj murder case of 2014—the rumours have it that Manoj, who was from a CPI(M) family, had been warned several times by Jayarajan not to associate himself with the RSS.[11]

Similar charges are hurled by the CPI(M) at RSS workers, including the late E. Manoj and P. Sasidharan, who is now the RSS's *vibhag karyavah* (a position in between the state and district levels)[12] of Kannur. Manoj—an accused in multiple murder cases—was lynched fifteen years after his alleged involvement in the attack on Jayarajan, on a day when Mohan Bhagwat, the chief of the RSS, and the BJP president Amit Shah were in Kerala.

I met Jayarajan within a week of Manoj's killing. After the interview, I carried my laptop to a beachside restaurant in Kannur and penned the first few lines of my dispatch for *Open* magazine:[13]

Communist Party of India (Marxist) leader P Jayarajan welcomes you with a disarming smile, as if he is meeting a comrade-in-arms after decades. Long years of pain and suffering following an attempt on his life by Rashtriya Swayamsevak Sangh rivals have not dented his sense of humour and hearty laugh, nor his enthusiasm for exchanging pleasantries. Neither does he seem overly distracted by the political turmoil building up in the aftermath of the murder of 42-year-old local RSS leader E Manoj, which could put several of his party workers in the dock. He would rather enjoy the pleasant yet unrelenting rain outside. He goes on to crack a joke or two about Rahul Gandhi, pokes fun at the naïveté of expelled former CPI(M) MP AP Abdullah Kutty, who has found sanctuary in the Congress, and inquires about national politics and Modi with the curiosity of a teenager. He then picks up a call with his left hand— he can barely move the other one—to brief his lawyers about the latest criminal cases slapped on party workers in this northern Kerala district that has been a simmering pot of political violence for long. Someone mischievous or subversive just had to open the lid, and all hell would break loose.

Jayarajan is back in chat mode as soon as he hangs up the phone. In between explaining the nature of the cases against his party workers, he talks about his exercise regimen: he goes for a brisk walk every day. That is all. At 64, he is still youthful and jovial despite having to live with a right arm rendered immobile and with numerous other scars.

Manoj was a prominent RSS functionary in the district when his vehicle was first bombed before he was hacked to death, during the Onam season. A local CPI(M) leader had told me then that comrades in Kathiroor couldn't stomach the fact that P. Jayarajan had to flee from Kathiroor, while Manoj, who was among the accused and who they claim was part of the group of assailants, roamed around freely. Much to the embarrassment of the Marxists, Jayarajan's son, Jain, put up a Facebook post congratulating Manoj's killers, further sparking hostilities and exposing the deep sense of revenge. Though the post was deleted, the then state secretary of the RSS in Kerala, Gopalankutty Master, told me in an interview that he believes that the killing was done with the blessings of CPI(M)'s top leadership.

It is rather obvious to state that Manoj wasn't the first victim of retributive politics after the murder attempt on Jayarajan. P.P. Suresh Babu almost made it to that list in 1999, months after Onam.

In November 1999, Suresh Babu boarded a morning bus from his home at Kavumbhagam in Thalassery heading for Kannur. He was on his way to his office in the district collectorate. He noticed some people, familiar faces, on the bus, carrying big shopping bags, but didn't pay much attention because buses are always full of familiar faces and people carrying shopping bags. Yet, something seemed amiss for Babu, and he was glad that he reached his office safely some time later.

Around lunchtime, he saw the same men on the vast collectorate campus, at least two of them still carrying those bags. Towards early evening, they were still there; some of them had moved closer to the staircase. By the time Babu had his evening chai, some more people had gathered around the three staircases on all sides of the long corridor leading to his upper-storey office. Until then, he had assumed these men had come for some work in the collector's room or the ancillary offices. As the clock ticked by, his gut instinct told him that they weren't there for any usual work. Still, his rational mind stayed in denial mode, and he wondered why anyone would come after him. There were no cases against him; neither had he been part of any criminal conspiracy against a political rival.

But his instinct won, and he decided against going downstairs. He called up a few police officers, some of whom agreed to take action. But when nobody turned up even after an hour, he called up a senior officer again who directed the special branch (town) circle inspector P.P. Unnikrishnan to rush to the spot. Babu was given a blunt message: 'Don't leave the office.'

The police arrived in three batches to nab the suspicious hangers-on and confiscated whatever was inside the bags. It included bombs, swords and axes. A suo motu case of attempting to kill Babu was registered, and the case is still pending in the high court.

Anyone less vigilant than Babu—whose family has long been associated with the RSS, including with the likes of the late Bhaskara Rao, Kerala's *pranth pracharak* (the designation of the all-powerful RSS nominee of the Nagpur headquarters who calls the shots in the state)—would have paid with his life. I remember Babu from the 1990s in Sree Narayana College, where we were both students. He was much leaner then, an ABVP leader who walked in brisk strides. He is currently a state-level office-bearer and one of the topmost leaders of the RSS in Kannur.

It wasn't that K.T. Jayakrishnan Master was any less vigilant. A month after Suresh Babu was targeted, his fellow RSS leader, Jayakrishnan Master was slashed to death by assailants inside a classroom full of students in a school in Mokeri, which falls in the Thalassery tehsil. Shortly after P. Jayarajan was ambushed inside his own home, Jayakrishnan Master's name had come up for discussion in political circles as the brain behind the assault. With intelligence reports suggesting a counter-attack on him, he had been assigned police security. On 1 December 1999 at around 10.35 a.m., while Jayakrishnan Master was conducting a class, his bodyguard went for a toilet break (apparently, according to RSS sources, the man deliberately went missing for a while). It was all the time a mob of killers needed to barge into the classroom and knife him to death in the most brutal fashion, as forty-two eleven-year-olds watched in horror and shock.[14]

Prajeesh N.K., then a college student, was close to Jayakrishnan Master and had met him the night before his death, along with a few others, when they chatted casually about life and politics. The next morning, he was devastated to know of Jayakrishnan Master's murder in the classroom.

Prajeesh, eighteen years later, is no longer associated with the RSS. He has come under the spell of Karunakara Guru and takes part in ashram activities. But, at the request of a colleague, he accompanies me to Jayakrishnan Master's home, along with local RSS leader Jayadevan. Shanta Kumar, Jayakrishnan Master's brother, greets me cordially at the traditional, single-storey Kannur house set at the end of a winding, tree-lined lane that—inappropriately—displays the red flag of the CPI(M) at its entry point. It is evident that the flag has been put there to spite the family.

In the Jayakrishnan Master murder case, A. Pradeepan, a local CPI(M) leader, and six others were arrested. One of the accused committed suicide during the trial, one was acquitted and five were sentenced to death by a sessions court. The high court upheld the judgment. The Supreme Court later acquitted four of them, and only Pradeepan stayed in prison. In 2011, Pradeepan was released by the state's Left Democratic Front (LDF) government, in line with the practice of political parties waiving the sentences of its cadres, using loopholes in the law or lack of sufficient proof. A year later, he was elected president of the parent–teacher association in the very school where Jayakrishnan Master was slain.[15]

Kumar heard about his older sibling's death when he stepped out to have coffee with a friend in Thalassery town. He used to maintain an office there, conceptualizing building plans for clients; these days, he is setting up mobile towers for cellular companies. He is bitter about the policies of the CPI(M), which, he says, hinge on violence. He has never been politically aligned with any party, but argues that the CPI(M) will cease to exist if they shed any more blood. According to him, it is the supremacy of violence that binds the CPI(M) as one entity in the district and elsewhere. His late father, Ananthan Master, also a schoolteacher like his older brother, used to be a CPI(M) activist. The fact that a man from a CPI(M) 'family' became an RSS worker angered the Marxists the most, says Kumar, cracking sarcastic jokes about CPI(M) leaders such as Pinarayi Vijayan, Kodiyeri Balakrishnan and P. Jayarajan. Age has embittered Kumar, who has four more siblings. Kausalya, his mother, watches from a distance, and makes a kind gesture of acknowledgement of a visitor at home. She offers a beatific smile, allowing her silence to make her statement, and retreats into the inner rooms.

Jayakrishnan Master, says Jayadevan, became an active member of the RSS after he shifted temporarily from Kannur to Chengannur in the Alappuzha district of South Kerala to do his teacher's training course in 1982. When he started working at the Mokeri Upper Primary School near Panoor, he faced threats for 'intruding' into Marxist turf. 'He was targeted because he was popular among young people here,' says his brother.

Jayakrishnan Master's political rivals, however, don't speak as fondly of him. Neither do members of the Congress and the policemen in the district. A policeman told me that the late RSS leader, who was a senior state-level leader of the BJP's youth wing, apparently, had an unsavoury background and was vitriolic in his comments against opponents. P.K. Premnath, a youth-wing leader of the CPI(M), had a few years ago referred to Jayakrishnan Master as a 'bushy-moustachioed man' with a criminal past,[16] who went to classrooms with a knapsack containing an S-shaped knife.[17] He was trained to kill and had meticulously planned attacks on CPI(M) members, Premnath had alleged, adding that Jayakrishnan Master was the kingpin of killer squads that had routinely carried out ambushes on CPI(M) cadres.

True, the attack on Jayakrishnan Master wasn't an unprecedented one by Kannur standards. As I look into district police records and conduct interviews with police officers, I find out that E. Raju Master of the CPI(M) was killed by RSS men in front of his students on his way back from school; his killing took place on 26 October 1978, outside the Panoor Lower Primary School. In 1972, the CPI(M) leader P. Damodaran Master was hacked in front of his students in the Vilakkottur Lower Primary School near Panoor. A month before the attempt on Jayakrishnan Master, V.K. Suresh Babu of the CPI(M) and teacher at Thalassery's St Joseph's School had a narrow escape after being attacked in front of his students by RSS-backed men.

Jayakrishnan Master's brother and friends are distraught at what they call the character-assassination campaign against him, which includes expletive-laced slogans raised by the CPI(M) workers, saying he ought to be left alone at least in death.

The 'Master', the other one, who lived to tell the tale did so without his limbs below the knees.

I remember that distant night in Thazhe Chovva, 6 kilometres south of Kannur town, from where a vehicle had departed in the evening to settle an issue 'elsewhere'. It had been reported through the CPI(M) channels to some of the 'handlers'—those who controlled a band of toughies trained for 'self-defence' by the party. Back then, most of them were a constellation of autorickshaw drivers, beedi workers or hardcore partymen with a background in martial arts. These days, they are mostly tipper drivers—a vehicle also called *naikurukkan* in Kannur thanks to its peculiar shape, a hybrid of a dog and a fox.

Several policemen who have held senior positions in the district of Kannur tell me that, in most cases, men are picked up randomly from various parts of the district, given fake names and put together as a killer squad. The purpose is that even if some of them are caught by the police, the identity of the others shouldn't come to light. Most people would have met for the first time and even the 'handler' may not reveal his own name.

But on the evening of 25 January 1994, the people who had left in a vehicle for a 'mission' must have been known to each other—they were mostly from around there, all associated with the CPI(M). Around 8.30 p.m., they overpowered a political rival who had disembarked from a bus near the Mattanur area of the district, chopped off his limbs below the knees, burst a few bombs to scare away the crowd, and made good their escape. The reason for the attack was that the man, Sadanandan Master of the RSS, had got one of his own relatives, a CPI(M) branch secretary, badly beaten up at dawn near the Mattanur bus stand—the victim now walks around with a limp.

The early morning assault on the CPI(M) local leader followed a heated exchange of words between him and Sadanandan Master, a well-built, charismatic man who was then employed in a lower primary school, where he had allegedly enticed children from CPI(M) families to attend religious rituals, an unpardonable offence from a Marxist point of view. Sadanandan Master himself had had a leftist excursion during his college days though he was an active Sangh worker before and after that. His late father, Kunjiraman Nambiar, had been a CPI(M) worker, as were some of his uncles. But Sadanandan Master veered back towards the Sangh ideology after Malayalam poet Akkitham's article, *'Bharata Darshanangal'*, in the *Mathrubhumi* weekly blew his mind, around the mid-1980s. It helped him realize that the 'RSS's idea of cultural nationalism was more suited to our state's natural ethos rather than the Marxist interpretation of how society should be'.[18]

He was only thirty when he lost his legs to violence and now uses prosthetic legs. After the attempt on his life, he later shifted to Thrissur district where he became a teacher of social science at a higher secondary school. Step by step, Sadanandan Master rebuilt his life, both politically and personally. He is married to Vanitha Rani, also a teacher, and has a daughter who is an engineer. In 2016, he returned to Kannur and contested as a BJP candidate from the Koothuparamba assembly constituency. Though he lost, he attracted nationwide attention due to the RSS's campaign blitz that saw various Sangh sympathizers landing in Kannur to work for him and talk about the story of his life as a survivor.

While Sadanandan Master, the former *jillahsahakaryavah* (district secretary) of the RSS, was being taken to hospital, he sang patriotic songs to fight back the pain. Around the same time, allegedly, RSS volunteers slayed K.V. Sudheesh,[19] a leader and a rising star of the SFI, right in front of his elderly parents in a relatively RSS-dominated area in the district called Thokkilangadi.

As a friend, I knew very well that Sudheesh had no idea he would be the target of a murderous attack. He was convinced that being a mere student leader, and one who was friends with all the RSS workers in the region, he would never be targeted. So he ignored warnings from party colleagues, advising him to shift to a 'safer' location. He was all of twenty-seven years old and, in January 1994, had been recovering from injuries caused by a police lathi charge months earlier—he had been mercilessly beaten during picketing at the district collectorate.

In a bitter twist of irony, those very RSS friends were part of the group that stormed into his humble home on the night of 25 January, just hours after Sadanandan Master was attacked, to butcher him to death as his parents wailed and begged them to spare their young son.

The next morning I woke up to a call from a CPI(M) activist, K.V. Sudheesh. He broke the ugly news to me that Sudheesh[20] had been killed inside his home by RSS men, adding that he had personally made the call to assure me that it wasn't he—a namesake—who had been killed. I headed for the Thalassery government hospital mortuary where a hospital staffer lifted the bed sheet that Sudheesh was covered with. It was a mangled mass of flesh and blood. Any display of shock or emotion would have been scorned by the comrades present, so I shut down the wrenching response in my gut, walked out, lit a cigarette, and inhaled viciously.

It was the first of several macheted bodies I would see in my life.

Sudheesh's parents then shifted to the house of their daughter elsewhere in the district. I met one of his brothers-in-law there a year after his death. He told me he imagined Sudheesh had gone somewhere for higher studies. 'I can't believe that he is no more.'

In the process of writing this book, I sent an interview request through a common friend to Sudheesh's sister, and she declined. I immediately understood: coping with grief is easier said than done, even twenty-three years later.

In Kannur, though, such tales have lost their sting.

4

The Spell of the Northern Ballads

The tales of woe today could have been heroic fables in another century.

Like cattle overfed by the meat industry, there was a class of people in Kannur for over a thousand years—until about a hundred years ago—who were trained to acquire exceptional martial-arts skills for the sole purpose of either winning or dying in disputes between local kings. Most of these disputes were frivolous quarrels. For instance, if a local king stared at or mocked another, the incident would call for a sparring between the Chekavars whom they hand-picked for a duel in exchange for a few bags of rice or clothes. The winner of such kamikaze-like missions might even earn some jewellery. To perpetuate this tradition, the dead and the victors in such confrontations, which took place in full public view, were remembered in heroic songs called the Northern Ballads.

Winning was heroism. So was dying.

While a large section of pundits dismiss the linkage between the traditional past and the spree of violence today, statistics show that even within Kannur, it is areas that were once mentioned in the Northern Ballads that have seen disproportionately high levels of bloodbath. Traditionally, the Chekavars were trained in kalaripayattu and readied for engaging in angams meant to uphold the honour of their princelings or wealthy local kings. The practice was widespread in a region formerly called Kadathanadu and nearby areas where kalaripayattu training was more of a habit than a sport. If two princes announced a spar, their hired Chekavars would face each other until one of them died in a duel involving swords and sparring with weapons such as *urumi* (whiplike blades) and multi-bladed urumis. In the nineteenth century, for a long period, the British banned the practice of kalaripayattu after the East India Company's forces were hobbled by these soldiers' gravity-defying skills in the service of a local king, Pazhassi 'Lion of Kerala' Raja, which helped him win surprising victories against them in the late eighteenth century.

The majority of the victims—and the perpetrators—of conflicts were from the Thiyya caste. In fact, many Thiyya families today trace their roots to this Chekavar lineage, and to mythological fighters such as Aaromal Chekavar and

Unniyarcha (of the Puthooram family), the much-revered female warrior with extraordinary martial-arts skills.

The Chekavars, notwithstanding their expertise in such duels, remained marginalized through history, though a spate of movies made in the last century glorified their lives and their loyalty, and embellished their lifestyle. The earlier movies had stuck to the traditional folklore, such as the one where Aaromal's cousin cheats and gets the great warrior killed. In the late 1980s, the movie *Oru Vadakkan Veeragatha* overturned this belief prevalent in the Northern Ballads, and was an instant box-office hit thanks especially to its dialogues and cast. Written by renowned writer M.T. Vasudevan Nair (MT) and starring national award-winning actor Mammootty, the film's interpretation was that Chandu, Aaromal's cousin, was in fact a genius and was portrayed in a bad light in the ballads because he was a poor cousin. MT featured Aaromal as the privileged cousin with inferior martial-arts skills compared with Chandu—it was a case of Karna being the hero instead of Arjuna. The movie was a culture shock to me and other youngsters at the time, though we loved watching it.

I also remember an inebriated uncle singing paeans to Aaromal: '*Paadaam, paadaam Aaromal Chekavar pandankam vettiya kathakal, veera kathakal, dheera kathakal, athbhutha kathakal paadam . . .*' These are lyrics from a song sung by Yesudas and Jayachandran in a 1972 movie, *Aaromalunni,* which can be translated as: 'Let's sing the songs of Aaromal Chekavar's memorable duels, those heroic tales, of those miraculous feats . . .'

It wasn't just the Chekavars who learnt kalaripayattu; men like Thacholi Othenan (of the Thacholi Manikkoth family) and others were gurus to hundreds of kalaripayattu exponents, the majority of whom belonged to a freer and relatively well-off community. The upper-caste Nambiars of today claim to be their descendants. Yet, it was the Chekavars who were called upon to fight the frivolous angams to 'save the honour of' the kings and princelings for over a thousand years. It is a pretty easy guess that the more privileged practitioners of kalaripayattu didn't want to die over trivial ego clashes.

Be that as it may, learning kalaripayattu has been a childhood preoccupation with families in and around the Thalassery region and that included my father's home village in Pattiam—many of my cousins made it a point to learn it even in the late twentieth century, before gyms and far-eastern martial-art forms encroached on to a turf that was exclusively kalari's. Karate and kung fu spread as fads in northern Kerala within a decade of Bruce Lee's death.

One of the most remarkable takeaways from kalari classes is that whatever you learn is not to be misused. 'Pray that you never will have to fight a person and use techniques learnt here,' the *aasan* (master) reminds you at each class. It can be compared with far-eastern martial arts such as kung fu, which was treasured and taught in ancient China, not only for the physical aspects—defence of one's nation, physical exercise, preventing illness, promoting longevity, and so on—it was also a means to instil moral behaviour, teach a life philosophy and be a tool for aesthetic expression. In the same vein, kalaripayattu was meant to instil self-discipline, enhance mental focus and build character. There are those who still believe that kalaripayattu should be taught far more widely to bring down the level of violence in Kannur by inculcating among the younger generation a sense of responsibility and mental control.

But—just as Bolo, the villainous character in Bruce Lee's *Enter the Dragon*, misused his strength and kung fu training to hurt and maim—centuries of misuse of skills acquired from kalaripayattu for promoting a mercenary culture in some parts of North Kerala have had huge consequences.

Overcoming fear had been an obsession in my childhood spent among the Marxist revolutionaries of Kannur, which had in previous decades seen massive repression of the leftists by Congressmen, the police and the state. Many kalaripayattu exponents have thrown their weight behind the fledgling band of communists since the 1940s; in many parts of the region, small groups of party cadres would batter landlords, Congress troublemakers and their police lackeys into submission. 'The communists had to resist attacks on them, especially on hapless women in their households who were singled out for attack because the men were mostly away, underground. It was largely due to those kalaripayattu wizards who organized squads of volunteers and trained them to resist that the opponents backed off,' says P. Jayarajan, district secretary of the CPI(M). It is part of communist legend that in places like Kayyur and Karivellur and across the Thalassery region, martial-arts exponents had resisted attempts to physically eliminate the communists in the early decades of their party's formation in North Kerala.

Babu, a kalaripayattu aasan from Eramam in Payyanur, tells me that his father, martial-arts expert Narayanan Nambiar, like various others before him, had helped the undivided communist party in the face of relentless attacks from goons allegedly hired by the Congress to crush the party at a time when it had launched several peasant movements in the district.

I remember visiting a kalari near my father's home at an age when I wasn't yet ready for school. It had only male students, though other kalaris around Kannur trained young women too. My role was to watch as my cousins stripped down as soon as they entered the kalari, applied coconut oil all over their bodies and changed into *langotti*s, a diaper-like loincloth—a laughable sight back then. Sitting on the sidelines, we little ones often had to fight back our mirth at seeing older cousins underdressed, because the aasan of the kalari was a strict man who brooked no nonsense. The students would start off with a prayer to mother earth before saluting the kalari devi, who is Durga herself. We, the young, were all there because we had to learn kalaripayattu, step by step, and had to shape our mind and body to suit the practice of this ancient martial-art form, which, we were told, was the father of all martial arts, including karate, kung fu and judo. It wasn't just a morning ritual; it was a way of life, like yoga. The elders offered us pieces of advice—if you become a fine practitioner of kalaripayattu, you become fearless and far more mature than others your age.

Babu, the kalaripayattu aasan, is convinced that the centuries-old hired-gun culture of the Chekavars is the anthropological cause for the clashes that continue to grip the region as cadres of opposing political groups fight each other over either retaining or winning a political foothold. While murder rates in Kannur are lower than most other Kerala districts, politically motivated murders are the highest here. Babu says that as a trainer, like his father before him, he had noticed that the numerically preponderant Thiyya community in North Kerala exhibits what he calls higher levels of *rajogunam*, or ferocity, compared with other castes, including his own, the Nambiars, who have also traditionally practised and taught kalaripayattu. He then offers a caveat, 'I am saying this from my experience of interacting with my students and by generally observing society from the point of view of someone who knows a bit about physical and mental aggression and the role of martial arts in it.'

However, historian Rajan Gurukkal disapproves of using references from the Northern Ballads to tie them to the violence as a 'cultural phenomenon'. He tells me that he considers the skirmishes and brutal killings in the district to be a mere law-and-order issue.

I spoke to S.R.D. Prasad, a Kannur-based kalaripayattu teacher and the author of an encyclopedia on the martial-art form. He looks at the region's violent past differently. He states that killing and dying to settle a dispute between chieftains or local kings were part of the judicial system of the day. He is of the view that the Chekavars played a significant role in society in those days. 'Thanks to them, the rest of the subjects of the two kings who had fallen out over an issue did not have to fight each other. Nor was there a scope for a war in which many people would get involved. The Chekavars alone fought in a duel and decided the outcome [like the Samurais of Japan, the Chekavars believed in honour, and would choose death over the humiliation of losing]. There is an absurdity in that when we look at it from the current human rights' point of view, but the system of the time minimized deaths.'

Taking a historical perspective throws up another theory to explain the political violence in the district. The northern parts of Kerala saw social-identity quests as a result of the militant peasant movements in the 1930s and 1940s—which had a tendency to use violent means to counter violent repression—as opposed to Kerala's south where the political culture was based on social and caste reforms influenced by spiritual leaders such as Sree Narayana Guru, Ayyankali and Chattambi Swamikal.

If one seeks it, there's compelling proof of the parallels between the modern-day political clashes and the ancient Chekavar tradition. A Congress leader of the district says there is often revelry that follows a killing, making it similar to triumphant jubilations of the winning side after an angam. The CPI(M) had alleged that when K.V. Sudheesh was kept in the mortuary of the Thalassery government hospital in 1994, his political antagonists allegedly cheerfully distributed sweets next to the nearby Westend restaurant. Throwing down the gauntlet is another notable feature of these political spars—as it is in fierce martial-arts combat. From P.R. Kurup of the PSP, whose party had some influence in some pockets of Kannur in the 1960s and the 1970s, especially in Panoor, to MVR in his initial avatar as a CPI(M) stalwart, to N. Ramakrishnan of the Congress, to Kodiyeri Balakrishnan of the CPI(M), Kannur has seen politicians throwing open challenges to their rivals in a stark display of masculinity in politics. Most of them engaged in rabble-rousing speeches. The RSS and the BJP too have not been far behind. An RSS leader stated that they should stop targeting bulbs and aim for the transformers, suggesting that his organization should eliminate leaders and not just grass-roots workers of the rival parties. This declaration was followed by the attack on P. Jayarajan. Jayakrishnan Master himself had made a speech before his death that the RSS would accomplish its mission to bump off Jayarajan, who had escaped an attempt on his life by the skin of his teeth.

Dr T. Sasidharan, head of the political science department at Sree Narayana College and author, has written extensively on the Kannur violence, and why the district is different from others in Kerala. He has authored the first research-based account of the roots of the political violence and the role that *kudippaka* (vendetta) plays in this. In his essay 'Kudippaka in Kannur Politics: An Investigation',[1] he writes, 'Religious leaders have the least sway here. Political leaders literally set the agenda even in . . . daily life.' His explanation is that Kannur's rich legacy of temple art (*theyyam*), belligerent deities (*ugramurti*s), and theyyam idols (Wayanad Kulavan, Kathivannur Veeran, Muthappan, et cetera) have their origins from common people who were martyrs in the fight against feudalism. He posits that the temples, or *theyyakavu*s, were perhaps the first memorials to martyrs.

Spiritually inclined folks look at all this a tad differently, though—they do acknowledge the role of kudippaka, but then link it to something far more mystical and ancient. They are of the belief that the bloodshed and hatred in the region today is an outcome of centuries of the Chekavar tradition— which allowed young, able-bodied men to martyr themselves for stupid reasons. A section of them also believe that the disquiet in the district is due to the 'wandering souls of the dead' who have found no redemption. My wife, a North Indian practitioner of Buddhism, muses that it may have to do with the 'karma of the land'. The contention is that not all phenomena can be demystified using modern research methodologies and social and political tools of analysis.

Rationalists—including myself, I must add—may dismiss such assertions, but several highly educated politicians and a few notables in Kannur tell me that 'divine intervention' is the need of the hour. While they don't wish to name themselves for fear of being judged by a highly literate society, they contend that such efforts are already on the anvil—such as mystics performing suitable rituals to foster peace in the region—and that there are indications that the violence would decline over the next few years, especially after it has become a national debate and a much-reported issue, forcing the police to swing into action.

The argument they put forth is that *vasana*, a product of past actions, impels karma, present action. Those who indulge in violence have such traits or karmic compulsions stored in their cells and such tendencies or desires propel further action in the form of violence. Though such theories can easily be categorized as unscientific, even former top cops such as Alexander Jacob argue that the roots of violence in Kannur between the RSS and the CPI(M)—which is less than fifty to seventy years old—lie in the existence of a martial culture in the ancient past. One could associate it with twentieth-century Swiss psychiatrist and psychoanalyst Carl Jung's theory of the collective unconscious—the part of the mind containing memories and impulses that originate in the inherited structure of the brain, and are common to a community or mankind as a whole.

Swami Sayoojya Nath Jnana Tapaswi, who is originally from Valliyayi, close to violent Panoor, says that he is aggrieved at seeing many of his close friends and associates perish. As a child, he would be devastated to know about each death in his locality, but it was only after he joined the Santhigiri Ashram, set up by Shri Karunakara Guru, that he began to realize why his guru suggested prayers and reparatory measures to bring some solace to Kannur. His guru passed away in 1999, but he had shared with his disciples the details of the curse haunting Kannur: in the microworld that is invisible to the human eye, *antharyamikal*, or microforms, of those killed in violence (including in angams) infest the atmosphere around. 'Jesus Christ called such forces Satan, and Prophet Muhammed jinns,' says Sayoojyanath. To ward off their evil influence, the guru had initiated a process that started at the homes of his disciples so that they didn't go astray. The process continues, he says.

He adds that it is when nations become spiritually weak and distorted that countries wage wars for generations, like they do in Afghanistan and parts of the Middle East. 'What we do is *pithrushudhdhi* [purifying the souls of the ancestors],' he says. His explanation is that most Chekavars who fought duels died for no good reason, and so they are unsettled even after death by a lack of purpose. 'Because the ancestors tend to be in *neech rashi* (inauspicious coordinates), they beget unstable children. It is an endless cycle,' he adds, emphasizing that the ashram is taking small steps towards purging the district of the curse.

A survey of more than several dozen people around Panoor and in my family, most of them highly educated, prove that Swami's faith in the supernatural and the mystic is contagious.

5

The Flag-Bearers

Returning to more earthly matters, the militant peasant and labour movements of North Malabar have contributed immensely to the shaping of Kannur's political culture.

To understand the legacy of the Left and its current coordinates (as well as its disequilibrium), it is crucial that we probe the political climate in the region and its leaders, some of whom were intrepid revolutionaries who redefined the political and social landscape of the district. As Marx himself reminded us, 'Men make their own history, but they do not make it as they please.' Communists in India have historically been painted by rivals as troublemakers, and criticized for their violent means, but it is important to remember that the movement began when caste and class discrimination in

India was still extreme—notwithstanding the raging freedom movement, the lower castes faced daily humiliation, violence, rape and abuse—and militancy was one of the very limited, if not the only, recourses that the poor and low caste could have taken against their wealthy, upper-caste oppressors. Of all places in Kerala, caste supremacy and repression of workers were unchecked in North Malabar around the time of the beginning of the communist movement in India.

A chain reaction of agrarian unrest—as well as factory strikes—followed the formation, in 1934, of a pro-socialist caucus within the Congress party at the national level, named the Congress Socialist Party (CSP). Some key left-oriented leaders from the state who joined the CSP were destined to lead the farmer struggles from the front. Mahatma Gandhi, who remote-controlled the Congress, had famously disapproved of the CSP's ways. His argument was that the class struggle, as prescribed by socialist and communist leaders across the world to ensure a more just society, would result in violence. For Gandhi, non-violence was the cornerstone of his anti-British campaign and political agitation, which came to be known as satyagraha.

The CSP became active in states such as the United Provinces[1] and many parts of East India much before it began to pick up momentum in Kerala. The early leaders of the CSP included Acharya Narendra Dev, Jayaprakash Narayan, Minoo Masani, Professor Abdul Bari, Purushottam

Trikamdas, Sampurnanand, Ram Manohar Lohia, N.G. Ranga, E.M.S. Namboodiripad and Achyut Patwardhan. The socialists within the Congress had been active since the mid-1920s and had the partial blessings of Jawaharlal Nehru, who secured the Congress's endorsement of the socialist programme at its Karachi session in 1931.

Besides EMS, prominent CSP leaders from Kerala included P. Krishna Pillai and A.K. Gopalan. According to several communist historians, as also EMS, it was after the formation of the CSP that the party colleagues started addressing themselves in India for the first time as comrades. Many of these CSP leaders would later become part of the communist faction formed in Kozhikode in 1937 and later the first Kerala unit of the Communist Party of India, established secretly in Parappuram, near Pinarayi, in December 1939. Krishna Pillai became the first secretary of the CPI's Kerala unit at the convention attended by ninety people here.

Even so, communism wasn't new to Kerala. The first proto-Marxist organization was the tiny Thiruvananthapuram-based Communist League of 1931, but it didn't make inroads in any part of the state. And the biographies of Lenin and Marx published in the previous decades had not evinced much interest in the absence of a well-knit organization.[2]

The CPI of the early 1940s was Leninist in its ideology and modelled on the Russian communist party, with a strong hierarchy. In many ways, it resembled the rigid structure of the

Catholic Church, and was tailored to help any organization survive internal wrangling and uprisings, if any ever arose, with minimal damage. Vladimir Ilyich Ulyanov, better known as Lenin, the founder of the Soviet Union, was simply the strongest opinion leader of his time for the socialists, especially after the October Revolution of 1917 in Russia. In India too, it was the success of the revolution in Russia that stimulated widespread interest in communism and socialism. Lenin was the ultimate radical and rebel without whom the second Russian revolution that replaced the Mensheviks would not have taken place, as the great columnist and writer Tariq Ali argues in his book, *The Dilemmas of Lenin*. He believed in the centralization of power, not essentially for personal reasons, but thanks to deep-rooted ideological convictions. A keen reader of Karl Marx, Lenin had a microscopic understanding of the existing communist view of the world, especially the German exile's reasoning of how the Paris Commune failed.

An armed rebellion by workers in Paris in March 1871 resulted in a government of sorts run by slaves who held power in the city for seventy-two days until the French rulers crushed it. Marx had hailed the revolt but had often stated that he preferred workers building up political and industrial strength gradually rather than staging immediate armed uprising against the state. In his analysis later, Marx pointed out that the lack of a centralized authority was one of the key reasons for the fall of the Paris Commune. Therefore, to address any such lacunae in the new government of Russia that overthrew the Romanov monarchy, Lenin created a communist party that had to be run according to the principle of democratic centralism. It meant that party members could discuss and debate issues freely but had to finally uphold the majority decision; the late Soviet leader had explained the whole concept thus: 'freedom of discussion and unity of action'. Over time, the party's leaders ended up wielding enormous influence thanks to its sheer command-and-control structure, leading to gross abuses of power.

In Kerala, especially in undivided Kannur, the party structure and the ultimate loyalty it demanded from its members gave leaders such as P. Krishna Pillai and A.K. Gopalan an opportunity to cultivate the values of sacrifice and devotion. They couldn't have done this in the Congress party, which, under Gandhi, wasn't opposed to the rich classes that had a powerful grip over the activities and freedom of their tenants and peasants. A minority though they were, the landlords held the reins of society and could order summary execution of whoever questioned them or demanded more pay or more grains. For Gandhi, the mission of settling such grievous inequities of Indian society had to wait until it became free. The Congress under him needed funds from the wealthy to fight the British Empire.

Earlier in their political careers, Pillai and Gopalan were Gandhi loyalists as Congress workers. Interestingly, when

Pillai took part in nationwide agitations as part of Gandhi's Salt Satyagraha in 1930, he was a diehard believer in non-violence as the sole method to forge ahead with India's freedom movement. But becoming a communist came with a makeover. He and Gopalan, popularly known as AKG, would navigate peasant movements, labour strikes and inter-party conflicts that buffeted North Malabar in the late 1930s and 1940s. While Pillai died of a snakebite in 1948 after leaving a large imprint on the politics of Kerala, AKG would continue to shape the modus operandi of the communist forces in the state, through the 1964 split that led to the formation of the CPI(M) and the Emergency that came later, until his death in 1977, the year that the Congress lost the national elections for the first time, under Indira Gandhi.

'Their style of functioning helped the party grow and leave a lasting legacy in undivided Kannur district [which covered Kasaragod and parts of Wayanad besides the current Kannur district],' explains Churayi Chandran, a former CPI(M) leader, Marxist scholar and Thalassery-based educationist who has closely watched the region's political dynamics.

Interestingly, Pillai, the man who launched numerous worker mobilizations against landlords and factory owners in undivided Kannur, was born in South Kerala, in Vaikom, Kottayam. By the age of fourteen he had lost his parents. In 1927, he left his home town for Allahabad to learn Hindi, and 'returned to work as an activist of Dakshin Bharatha Hindi

Prachar Sabha'.[3] But in no time he took a plunge into the vortex of the country's freedom movement drawn by Gandhi's call for civil disobedience, which resulted in the breaking of the new colonial salt laws. He took part in the Salt Satyagraha march from Vadakara in Kozhikode to Payyanur in early 1930. He was jailed around the time Gandhi was imprisoned for defying the salt laws until the British government brokered a deal with the Congress in favour of talks. Pillai was also released when political prisoners were set free in exchange for agreeing to round-table talks. In an excellent profile of the man, R. Krishnakumar says that Pillai resigned from the Rs 30-a-month job as a Hindi pracharak (who would teach Hindi to non-Hindi–speaking people) before he became a volunteer in the Salt Satyagraha march.[4] In 1932, Gandhi was jailed again on his return to India following the failure of the talks, and he restarted civil disobedience. By the time Gandhi began his fast unto death in 1932 inside the Yervada jail in Pune and entered into a truce with B.R. Ambedkar over the question of separate electorates for Dalits under the British communal award, Pillai had become disinterested in Gandhian politics. He began to veer towards socialism and took up workers' agitations. The reasons were stark and simple: he saw for himself the lack of appeal for the civil disobedience movement among the lower castes and the working classes—the majority of the population— of North Malabar where the senior Congress leaders and sympathizers were the affluent class. Though the Congress in Kannur had a legion of Gandhian volunteers, several of its functionaries at the lower rungs were unemployed young men with a tendency to choose knuckles over words to make a point. These ruffians were routinely used by the landlords to rough up workers—many of whom were communists and socialists—and at times kill them, as in the case of Moyarath Sankaran. These Congress workers also obstructed the meetings of opponents and disrupted their processions. It is no secret that they worked as spies for the police, especially after independence.

Pillai wanted to work for the 'Congress for the poor' and not for the 'Congress for the rich' (this was written in a postcard that Pillai sent from jail to a friend). Since 1933, though Gandhi immersed himself in various activities, including the uplift of the 'Harijans' (now called Dalits) and promoting rural industry, Pillai's knowledge of the Congress's grass-roots reality in Kannur left him disenchanted with the man he had idolized.

That explains his enthusiasm to work closely with the CSP.[5] Pillai had already taken part in the landmark efforts to make temples, a veritable centre of exclusion that practised caste hegemony, accessible to all. The Guruvayoor temple in Thrissur district is still one of Kerala's most famous temples. Back then, when Kerala was a collection of the Malabar region (under the British Madras Presidency) and the princely states of Kochi and Travancore princely states, the Kerala Pradesh Congress Committee (KPCC) called for an agitation to allow entry to all castes into the temple, which had for centuries, practised restricted entry. What became known as the Guruvayoor Satyagraha was led by K. Kelappan (also known as Kerala Gandhi), Pillai, A.K. Gopalan and others. Pillai would display his valour and recklessness by entering the temple and ringing the bell, the first non-Brahmin to do so. When Nair guards and assistants hired by King Zamorin of Calicut threw punches at him, he loudly ridiculed them, '*Ushirulla Nair maniyadikkum, echila perukki Nair avante purathadikkum.*' ('The bold Nair rings the bell, the crumbs-loving Nair beats his back.')

The satyagraha held in Vaikom temple preceded the one at Guruvayoor. Held between 1924 and 1925, it yielded minor results and non-Brahmins won the right to walk along the roads adjacent to the temple. Various social reformers such as Sree Narayana Guru, Ramasamy Naicker and Mannathu Padmanabhan were involved in this. Gandhi and Vinoba Bhave had come down to monitor the movement. T.J. Nossiter, however, writes in his stellar work, *Communism in Kerala: A Study in Political Adaptation*,[6] that the agitation ended in defeat dressed up as compromise. Even so, such campaigns finally prompted the maharaja of Travancore, Sree Chithira Thirunal, to announce the Temple Entry Proclamation—drafted by the renowned Malayali poet Ulloor S. Parameswara Iyer—in 1936, permitting people of all castes to enter the temples in his kingdom. Hailed as the Magna Carta for the region, the announcement was lauded by the likes of Gandhi and C. Rajagopalachari. Historian Romila Thapar notes that the agitation was born out of the extreme injustice done to the Dalits and that it was a key event in the civil rights movements during the freedom struggle. 'Untouchability and denial of the right to use public roads were an extremely shameful aspect of the then social order, though great people such as the Buddha had battled against social discrimination several centuries ago,' she says. According to her, Gandhi's non-violent weapon of satyagraha had been evolved from agitations such as Vaikom.

Pillai, by now a committed socialist and drawn to communism, would begin to focus on the militant peasant and labour movements. He started setting up workers' bodies and trade unions across Kerala like a man possessed. R. Krishnakumar writes: 'Between 1934 and 1939, nearly 80 local trade unions were organised industry-wise in almost all the urban centres of Kerala [under the leadership of Pillai]. In addition, two central trade unions, one each in Kozhikode and Kannur, and an all-Kerala trade union committee also came into being. The dynamic leader that he was, Krishna Pillai also took the initiative to organise factory committees in every company and to include even the most backward among the labourers to bargain collectively for their rights.' The writer also brings out a facet of Pillai's political work which his comrade EMS pointed out later: 'Krishna Pillai was instrumental in dismantling the elitism ingrained in Kerala politics until then, and paved the way for its replacement by a collective leadership, especially of the working class and the peasants.'

Elitism in politics largely meant discounting issues of the working classes and the farmers. It was also marked by political work from a higher pedestal and leading by keeping a distance from the masses. Class bias was the most notable feature of such politics. Pillai revolutionized political work and, more often than not, had to operate clandestinely because mobilizing factory workers to demand higher pay or farmers to ask for more grain was illegal, and attracted strict punishment. A huge discontent had swelled in North Malabar where the Congress was relatively indifferent to the falling agricultural prices during the Depression and the years that followed.

De-eliticizing politics—or dismantling the hegemony or making politics egalitarian—also meant living among the farmers and labourers, and facing the potential brutality unleashed by the state against political activism then considered unlawful: such as organizing the millworkers and farmers to wage strikes or resorting to force against the exploitative and intimidatory landlords who had police support. Notionally upper caste (from the Nair community), but functionally from the working class, the well-travelled

Pillai was so driven by the spell of the new ideology that he had the element of a reckless adventurer about him. Though he was disciplined, committed and alert, yet the new mission—the emancipation of the working classes and the repressed peasantry—demanded that he become a fireball of an activist, a superman revolutionary, working overtime, covertly building an organization from scratch. The daunting challenges he took up made him a huge hit with the people he worked with, and invoked fear among the landlords and the police.

Nossiter says that few among the ninety founder members of the CPI in Kerala had any sophisticated knowledge of Marxism, but they enjoyed a valuable asset: a decade's immersion in the political and social movements of Malabar, Cochin and Travancore. That pronouncement was truer of Pillai than anyone else. In fact, in Malabar, the CSP had established units in each village except in the Muslim-dominated areas. It had also set up reading rooms and deputed local activists to spread literacy so as to introduce them to socialist publications. Making the communist party deeply entrenched at the grass roots was a superlative contribution by Pillai. He often travelled incognito, posing even as a beggar who slept on the street. The live wire that he was, he could make friends easily even with the sternest of people. For instance, in 1940, when EMS had to be sheltered from the British Police, Pillai had found for him at Mavilayi in Kannur the home of a toddy tapper named Nallikkandi Pokkan who hardly interacted with even his neighbours and was known for his brazen behaviour, especially with strangers. Pillai had struck up a friendship with Pokkan and though the government had announced a reward of Rs 1000 for information on EMS, he remained safe in Pokkan's home.

It is no surprise why Pillai found Kannur a fertile ground for launching peasant struggles. Kannur had seen extreme concentration of land among the upper castes, much more than any other district in the state (according to official data from the time). In Malabar, most of the land was held by the Namboodiris (in South Malabar) and Nairs (in North Malabar), though a section of rich Thiyyas did have large tracts of land in their possession as well. The majority of the poor lower castes were landless. In Travancore, the process of diffusion of ownership had been taking place since the 1950s and the trend continued. The trend in Kochi was similar to Malabar's.

Pillai, simply the first communist of Kerala, who began to be known by his pseudonym, *sakhavu* (comrade), was the brain behind the industrial strikes and farmer uprisings that would alter the political landscape of undivided Kannur forever. He not only had the nerve to distribute clandestine Marxist literature at the Lucknow session of the Congress party, but also earned the attention of the police for personally raising a hammer and sickle at an all-India labour conference held in Thrissur in April 1937.

Pillai had launched a raft of worker organizations and inspired clampdowns on the cotton mills of Kozhikode. He activated coir workers in Alappuzha who, some years later in 1946, spearheaded the Punnapra-Vayalar uprising—comprising mostly Ezhavas and Dalits—against the British-backed Travancore kingdom.

Yet, it was in undivided Kannur, far from his home town of Kottayam, that the impact of his political experiments would leave an indelible mark. He left his footprint on all political initiatives that turned out to be force multipliers to the growth of the communist party in the district. If there is one man who deserves credit for zealously spurring everyone into action—from weavers and beedi workers to peasants—it's Krishna Pillai. He was a peripatetic revolutionary, trundling from one village to another, and in the process, recruiting cadres and setting up safe homes for comrades forced underground.[7] He also sowed the seeds of various peasant movements in undivided Kannur, including Kayyur, Karivellur and Morazha, besides organizing textile mill strikes. Pillai was just forty-two when he died on 19 August 1948 while he was in an underground shelter at Kannarkattu in Alappuzha. His party had been banned after the then general secretary B.T. Ranadive's Calcutta Thesis, a call for an armed struggle against the Indian government, which a leftist scholar of the repute of Perry Anderson terms as 'insurrectionary'.

Krishna Pillai was hard-nosed, aggressive, tough and driven. He brooked no indiscipline within the party—in 1946–47, he had dismissed the state committee and created an ad hoc committee, much to the anguish of the central committee that overruled him. He was capable of taking such unilateral decisions. Those who stood against the duumvirate of EMS (on ideological and political issues) and Krishna Pillai (on organizational and practical questions) were ordered to follow its directions or face disciplinary action, according to Nossiter. Pillai[8] also advocated aggressive resistance against the repressive policies of the police and the ruling Congress, which unabashedly backed the landlords and industrialists. He was the shrewdest among his coevals and the legacy that he left behind in Kannur, one of his favourite stamping grounds, was a militant, well-knit organization spread across villages, cottage industries and textile mills. Nossiter states the obvious when he says that the communist cadres had earned a reputation for sincerity and simplicity even among their rivals.

And for unshakeable loyalty.

Born in 1904, A.K. Gopalan was two years senior to Krishna Pillai. According to communist lore, when both were CSP members, AKG is said to have lost his cool and slapped Pillai while engaged in an argument. An RSS veteran, R. Hari, recently narrated this story, hoping to shock me and also to put forth his contention that the undivided CPI, unlike his organization, the RSS, was a cadre-based party only in name. I had also heard this word-of-mouth story of the AKG versus Pillai stand-off from an early generation of communists. The truth was that, technically, AKG and Pillai were not yet CPI members, but CSP leaders. What is striking, though, is that Pillai didn't hit AKG back although he was fitter and stronger compared to his rotund senior. When I asked some senior leaders of the party about Pillai's reaction, they quoted him as saying to AKG, 'Gopalan, if I hit you back, pus will come out. I won't because I want you.' Pillai also deputed K.P.R. Gopalan, the legendary communist leader, to lure a sulking AKG back into the leftist fold in 1936 around the time of the 'hunger march' from Malabar to Madras. KPR got the job done.

AKG may have been impulsive by nature as a young man, but he had his ear to the ground when it came to people's anguish and agony. He had to snap ties with his landlord father who disapproved of his son's political activities, and had to seek help from others for food and lodging at a time when neither the Congress nor the fledgling communist party had the funds to take care of its full-time workers. Comrades like AKG had to stay with the poor, scrimp and save to travel on buses to do party work. Born in an upper-caste family, he worked among the Dalits, and at Kandoth in Payyanur, he was badly thrashed by members of the Thiyya community for 'trespassing' into their areas accompanied by Harijans. AKG, it is said, never recovered completely from that murderous assault. At a personal level, following the incident, his first wife was taken back to her home by her uncles because AKG had taken her along to a 'Harijan' neighbourhood.

Thanks to his rebellious nature, he was also the target of savage torture by the police before and after Independence. On the stroke of the midnight hour when Nehru was delivering his 'tryst with destiny' speech, AKG was in jail, serving yet another term, like he had in the prisons of various parts of India. These jail sentences and the ruthless assaults from the police, Congressmen and the private armies of landlords took a heavy toll on the health of a leader who had always led from the front without fear and with great ferocity. After Pillai's, it was AKG's style of working that his successors would emulate to the hilt inside the undivided party and later the CPI(M). Faced with the authoritarian ways of the Congress and their thuggish attacks, the communists had to resist.

AKG contended that his comrades were being targeted because the attackers could walk away with impunity. As part of self-defence, he formed what became famous as the 'Gopala Sena',[9] a team of volunteers trained in hand-to-hand combat and in using weapons. It was mostly due to this direction from AKG that in the 1950s, unlike the previous decade, any effort to target leftist cadres was met with stiff resistance.

For his cadres, AKG became one of the early mascots of strong-arm politics, though to people outside, he was a benevolent and avuncular figure who appeared out of the blue whenever there was any injustice against the poor. Like Pillai, he too took unilateral decisions to reach out to the downtrodden, and was often indifferent about party protocol in taking decisions before they were implemented. He was benign and warm, even to those who had chosen not to be part of the CPI(M) after the split in 1964. One former CPI member remembers that AKG walked 10 kilometres to attend his wedding near Chovva in Kannur though he had not invited him. The CPI leaders often say that the reason they could not muster people's support after the 1964 split was because AKG, the man who touched people's hearts, was on the other side.

Interestingly, P. Sundarayya, the first general secretary of the CPI(M), has narrated in his biography (translated into Malayalam as *Viplavapathayil Ente Yathra*—My Journey through the Revolutionary Path) how AKG, who didn't speak a word of Telugu, made a visit to the Telangana region where a peasant revolt (1946–51) had been crushed by the state forces, and struck an instant chord with the people who loved his benign appearance and disposition.[10] He was a regular figure at my home when I was an infant, and would pat my head in a fatherly way, I was told later. He gifted my mother a signed copy of his book, *In the Cause of People*, which, years later, I would carry with me to my boarding school to read and reread.

AKG also endeared himself to leaders of the stature of Pandit Jawaharlal Nehru, who enjoyed morning walks with him when he was prime minister and AKG the leader of the CPI's parliamentary group in the Lok Sabha. In an area of Kerala where social-reform–oriented caste organizations have had a comparatively lesser impact, it was peasant struggles and protests to obliterate caste atrocities, led by the likes of AKG, that helped the communist party forge ahead as an electoral force in the decades to come. In the process, AKG, revered for his organizational skills, began to be known as the 'crusader of the downtrodden'.

While the likes of AKG and Pillai who assiduously built a militant-cadre party would later be blamed for their competitive, masculine political posturing, the fact is it resulted in numerous peasant rebellions—from Kayyur to Kavumbai, and Kandikkai to Morazha—besides various other strikes that involved confiscation of rice during the famine years of the Second World War and serial strikes at the Aaron Mill, a textile unit in Kannur owned by the industrialist Samuel Aaron.

When AKG died in 1977, he was cremated at Payyambalam where hundreds of thousands of people came to pay tribute, including from far-off places in Andhra Pradesh. I have a vague memory of refusing to leave the beach because it was the largest sunset I had ever seen in my little life. As if the sun had come closer to witness its fiery scion finally lying still, and at peace.

A junior contemporary of Pillai and AKG, K.P.R. Gopalan too contributed immensely to transforming the communist party in the undivided Kannur district into a potent organizational entity, making deep inroads into Congress strongholds at a fast clip. The shrub *Chromolaena odorata*, which grows quickly, is called 'communist *pachcha*' in Malayalam, indicating that it spreads fast like communism. However, it would have been impossible for the comrades to bolster the party without resorting to force against the Congressmen. I remember one of my aunts, who was a senior leader of the women's wing of the CPI(M) telling me that '*ivide* party *adichundakkiyathanu* [the party was built here using brute resistance]'. What she meant was that in most parts of Kannur, the communists were under attack from the police and the Congress volunteers, who disrupted communist party meetings, processions and speeches. Even as late as the late 1970s, the SFI couldn't take out a procession in colleges, including the Sree Narayana College in the district, without being beaten up and dispersed by members of the KSU (Kerala Students' Union, the Kerala student arm of the Congress), says K. Sanil Kumar, a former

CPI(M) leader and former unit secretary of the SFI at Sree Narayana College. Things changed when a tough leader named T.P. Hareendran joined the college and began to hit back, even using knives. Very soon, the KSU workers stopped hurting the SFI boys, who were now free to organize activities of their choice.

History teaches us that the world over, violence has served certain functions to ensure justice in an unjust society. That was what drove Pillai, AKG and KPR to use organizational prowess to take on the bullying political rivals from the Congress who wanted to conserve the status quo favouring the rich landowners and upper castes. KPR, until he faced disciplinary action in the CPI(M) in the 1960s, symbolized his party's militant finesse. He was a hero to a generation of communists after he was captured in the Morazha agitation of 1940. It was an event organized by the state unit of the Congress (then dominated by the leftists) to protest against Britain joining the Second World War. In Morazha, things turned violent following clashes between the volunteers and the police, leading to the death of two cops. KPR was later sentenced to death in this case, but Gandhi intervened to ensure his release following nationwide protests. KPR himself had said self-effacingly that the real hero of the Morazha agitation was Araakal Kunhiraman, about whom not much can be found even in Marxist literature. Also, the several demands that the Morazha protesters raised have not often been highlighted. But such demands were indicative of the aggressive traits the communist party would display later.

In fact, the Morazha agitation was the first agrarian revolt in North Malabar. Its demands included: reparatory measures to handle the fluctuations in agricultural product prices; fair prices for agri products; and the punishment of officials who collected war funds forcibly. The agitations that followed in Kayyur, Karivellur, Kavumbai and other places, besides the Aaron Mill strike, would eventually step up the strength of the leftist forces and that of the communist party in North Malabar.

The Aaron Mill strike took place in two tranches, first in 1936 and then in 1939, placing the Left on a higher pedestal among the farmers and labourers in the struggles against the British and the exploitative industrialists and landlords. The mobilization of women, children, artists and others extended the communist party's sway over the region far and wide. KPR played a pivotal role in all these efforts.

M.V. Raghavan, unlike KPR and AKG who were from the *jenmi* (landlord) families, was born to an impoverished, notionally upper-caste family, similar to Pillai's. But unlike the founder-secretary, Raghavan never bothered to leave Kerala and explore India, and instead, he made a living doing odd jobs, including weaving. He had joined the party at a time when titans such as AKG, A.V. Kunhambu, KPR and Azhikodan Raghavan were at the helm of affairs in Kannur. C.H. Kanaran was the powerful state secretary when the party split in 1964 and the CPI(M) was formed. And within four years, Raghavan and a team of Young Turks had captured the leadership of the CPI(M) in Kannur in perhaps the first-of-its-kind effort to dislodge any high-level official panel of the party. Kunhambu, the leader who was at the forefront of the Karivelloor agitation, was the district secretary of the Kannur unit from 1964–67, the year he became part of the state secretariat of the CPI(M). Following which, KPR was named the district secretary. Within a few months, in December 1967, young leaders such as Arayakkandi Achuthan, M.V. Raghavan, Pattiam Gopalan and K.C. Nandanan came into the leadership through an unprecedented election replacing the official district panel. Azhikodan Raghavan, C.H. Kanaran and others were deeply shocked by the development. Soon, M.V. Raghavan consolidated his powers in the district, which was also due to the exit of KPR and the pro-Naxalite members from the CPI(M). He also had the blessings of A.K. Gopalan.

M.V. Raghavan brought to the fore a political culture that would have an impact on the CPI(M)'s Kannur unit for decades to come. Even as the party was growing organizationally, he never missed an opportunity to verbally assault his rivals in the most obscene manner, and often incited his cadres against their opponents. Party insiders say this constant display of aggressive masculinity was his way of ensuring his supremacy. Any dominance within the party of the intellectual kind would have diminished his appeal. Putting party cadres on a quasi-violent mode and on tenterhooks enhanced his persona as a belligerent leader with a halo around him. His street-fighting tactics, too, gave him an edge as he personally hurled abuse at the police at protest marches. People close to him, like the former member of Rajya Sabha Pattiam Rajan, say that his rivals hated him for his guts and for the fact that he never let an attack on his cadres go unpunished. Rajan argues that such measures acted as a deterrent against attacks on the CPI(M) cadre. I.V. Shivaraman, another close associate of MVR who was once a prominent leader of the CPI(M) in Kannur, says he has had disagreements with MVR, but what he admired about the man was his concern for the workers even at the grass roots. 'Their safety was of paramount importance to him. It was in his time as district secretary that the party grew manifold and the rivals started thinking twice about launching attacks on CPI(M) workers,' he tells me.

M.V. Govindan Master, the state secretariat member of the CPI(M), sees MVR as a leader who successfully expanded the party's influence and resisted attacks. Govindan Master talks about three phases in MVR's career: when he was a fiery CPI(M) leader; then a cantankerous opponent when he broke away and joined the Congress coalition during which time the Koothuparamba firing took place, killing several CPI(M) cadres; and later, his effort to reach out to the Left once again.

Roguishly handsome with an irresistible personality, MVR, who had a hardscrabble childhood, clearly used his toughie image to the maximum extent within and outside his party. Some of his contemporaries tell me that he was intensely competitive even within the party, a trait that was back then mostly associated with careerist Congress leaders. 'When the party decided to do something in an evening meeting, MVR did it that night itself, while others waited till the next morning. He competed tirelessly within the party; one-upmanship was his forte.'

MVR was no democrat.[11] On the contrary, he had a long history of purges and nepotism. He is known to have denigrated senior leaders, plotted their downfall, used his acolytes to publicly humiliate them, and had explored the immense possibilities of the craft of politically slaying an opponent within the Stalinist confines of his party, just as EMS himself often did. In the CPI(M) mouthpiece of Kerala, *Deshabhimani*, which at that time had very few editions, multiple photographs of MVR began to appear by the mid-1980s. But slowly, he would become unpopular among a section of the party leaders who hated not only his guts but also his puritanical, dictatorial tendencies.

MVR's craving for power was insatiable, and he had plotted to weaken the man who was the biggest threat to his vaulting ambitions: EMS, who was the first communist chief minister in the Indian republic, making Kerala the third place in the world where a communist government had been elected to power through an election, after San Marino and British Guyana. The first attempt by MVR's camp, it is said, was to open channels of communication with the West Bengal unit of the CPI(M), which wasn't mightily impressed with EMS's leadership in Kerala. Apparently, the late CPI(M) leader and EMS's contemporary, Jyoti Basu, was never a great admirer of EMS. By then, MVR and eight other leaders of the CPI(M) state panel had prepared what later came to be known as 'an alternative document' to the CPI(M) line that it would have no alliance with religion-oriented parties like the Muslim League. MVR and others, instead, favoured an alliance with the Muslim League, arguing that the CPI(M) could never do anything for the working classes unless it was in power, and that without the League's backing it was impossible for the Marxists to be in power in the southern state.

By the time this document was 'detected' by EMS and his then staunch ally, V.S. Achuthanandan, the CPI(M) had been out of power in Kerala since 1969 except for a brief spell in 1980. And by 1984, it appeared that the CPI(M)'s electoral prospects were very weak despite the party gaining in organizational strength, with MVR taking credit for the expansion of the party's base in the state. However, regretfully, he refused to take the blame for taking the party, especially in northern Kerala, down the violent course, engaging in an eye-for-an-eye bloodbath with its political rivals, both the Congress and the RSS. He also never apologized for the political atrocities and excesses under his watch. In hindsight, he was a sort of wartime leader who flourished in violent politics that rendered the moderate leaders within his party toothless. In fact, the late T. Kunhanandan Nair, a close friend of MVR's and a famous lawyer who helped the CPI(M) with various criminal cases when MVR was a powerful commissar, had warned him to end this 'farce of killings and counter-killings'.[12]

Ironically, MVR would see some of his former henchmen use similar tactics against him after his expulsion from the CPI(M), when he was aligned with the Congress-led United Democratic Front (UDF). The late CPI(M) local leader Poochali Gopalan of Kannur met MVR when the latter was a minister. MVR gave the nod for a proposal made by Poochali about a cooperative enterprise and suggested that he tell his party leaders (the likes of Pinarayi Vijayan) to be less rigid. Poochali, in an uncharacteristic repartee, told his former leader that it was he who had taught him and the CPI(M) in Kannur to be 'rigid'. Apparently, MVR just smiled in grudging approval.

Having held sway over the CPI(M) unit in Kannur from 1968–86, except for a brief period when he was jailed during the Emergency and from 1977–78, the damage that MVR inflicted on the party by sidelining peaceniks and grooming macho leaders has been beyond repair.

Some senior CPI(M) leaders still argue in favour of MVR's role in 'resistance' and 'political leadership' against the anti-CPI(M) atrocities unleashed by the Congress and the RSS, but their idol worship blinds them to the fact that M.V. Raghavan also added fuel to the dangerous fire of revenge and violence in northern Kerala.

6

Congress versus the Communists

In the late 1960s and '70s, M.V. Raghavan wielded enormous power within his party after he had managed to sideline—some say with A.K. Gopalan's covert help—senior leaders from trade unions (like in the case of C. Kannan) and farmer organizations (like in the case of A.V. Kunhambu), who were pivotal to the growth of the party in Kannur for more than three decades. In the run-up to the 1980s, many of his seniors and contemporaries who could have posed a threat to him either left the party, died or were killed, leaving him to deal mostly with yes-men and a small band of young rebels and old-timers who had to grin and bear the humiliation of his ruthless dominance, until an opportunity struck many years later.[1]

For the CPI(M), the slide in interest in peasant struggles and hard-line trade unionism was in line with the thinking among a section of the national party leaders, who largely believed that such activities tended to put the movement more on the revolutionary path while they were yearning to sail along the parliamentary route to power and formulate policy decisions for the disadvantaged and the marginalized. Alternatively, throughout India, communists were determined to place more emphasis on promoting student and youth feeder wings. With Indira Gandhi unofficially giving the nod for a large section of leftists to dominate the intellectual realm in exchange for leaving the political space to the Congress, such a shift in strategy, deliberate or otherwise, was irresistible.

Interestingly, MVR's brand of domination accompanied the decline of one brawny politician and the rise of another. And that gave no gap to experiment with peaceful political means, which would have meant ceding power to far more sober colleagues.

P.R. Kurup was a socialist leader who had made his entry into politics at the age of twenty in 1935. He claims in his autobiography, *Ente Naadinte Katha, Enteyum* (The Story of My Birthplace, and Mine), that he had fought feudal lords and their influence in his village. It is evident that he got attracted by socialism early in his life and had a band of supporters who would do anything for him. As a young man, he was charismatic and started off as a member and later as a leader of the PSP, a party formed by Jayaprakash Narayan after he disbanded the CSP. As decades went by, in a series of political shifts and realignments, he also worked with the Samyukta Socialist Party, Janata Party and the Janata Dal. Until the mid-1960s, he had been an anti-communist despite the fact that he had worked with some of them in the CSP (and maintained good relations with them, especially with P. Ramamurti, a founder politburo member of the CPI(M). Horror tales of people being thrashed by Kurup[2] or his supporters were endless in Panoor, Pathayakkunnu, Pathippalam, Pattiam, Kathiroor and other places. One of my paternal uncles once narrated to me how the men would arrive from nowhere and begin to beat up people, tearing off their shirts and mundus, and leaving before anyone could figure out what was going on. My uncle was one of the victims, not once, but on many occasions. The early 1980s saw Kurup's gradual eclipse in politics. Even so, during the summer vacations I spent in my paternal home during the time, it was a familiar sight to see aunts get into a huddle and whisper warnings such as 'Kurup's people are in Pathayakkunnu and they are heading for Kottiyodi'. Then they would dispatch a young adult from the family to find out what was going on. I remember occasions when some of my cousins had returned hurt from their reconnaissance.

Kurup's heyday as an anti-communist bully was in the 1950s and '60s, and other parties—such as the Congress, the

CPI and the Muslim League—had formed an 'action front', or a united group of sorts, for the sole purpose of taking on Kurup's goons who had a penchant for launching attacks on non-PSP workers at whim.

Notwithstanding such recklessness and the anti-communist rhetoric he was known for, over the decades, Kurup had no qualms about aligning with the communist bloc because nationally there were alliances between the PSP and the CPI(M). In the 1965 assembly elections, the CPI(M) did not announce a candidate for the Peringalam—Kurup's turf—constituency despite the obvious antagonism the party and its cadres had towards Kurup. But they had to respect the alliance that was in place. Besides, Kurup had proved to be a chameleon who could charm even the bitterest foe. Though the Left didn't make any commitment to vote for Kurup, the latter showed no hesitation in plunging into action by campaigning for CPI(M) candidates in nearby seats such as Thalassery. It is an altogether different matter that several PSP members, who weren't as politically agile as Kurup and were disillusioned with his new allegiance to their traditional rivals, proceeded to become members of the RSS or the Jana Sangh (or later the BJP).

Many areas where the PSP had some influence in Kurup's best years as an anti-communist became green pastures for the RSS to set up base since the socialists neither wanted to join the Congress nor the communists. The RSS became their natural option. For instance, Cheruvanchery near Pattiam, which now has considerable RSS presence, was once an influential spot for the PSP. One could name numerous other PSP strongholds in the district that, as if on cue, became RSS bastions or villages. While Kurup kept vacillating between an independent status, a pro-Left position and then pro-Congress and then back with the left front (in 1967, he was the cooperative, irrigation and *devaswam* (temple administration) minister in the CPI(M)-led EMS ministry, and in 1996, he was minister for forests and transport in the E.K. Nayanar ministry for three years), many of his cadres would part ways and join the RSS by virtue of being opposed to both the major fronts in the state. In that sense, alongside Kurup's[3] role in aggressively promoting the politics of violence in Kannur, his contribution towards grooming cadres who eventually ended up joining the BJP or the RSS is worth a thorough study.

Kurup, who continued to be part of the CSP under the leadership of Jayaprakash 'JP' Narayan until 1948, quit the CSP some months after Mahatma Gandhi's assassination. The provocation was a nationwide protest call by JP after the Congress veteran Sardar Vallabhbhai Patel spoke out against socialism at a meeting. And locally, like the communists, socialists like Kurup (who joined the PSP in 1952 after JP launched this new party), too, had to face attacks from the Congress toughies. Kurup, a kalaripayattu practitioner, has narrated in his biography many such encounters in which he displayed his physical prowess and agility to either browbeat or batter the vigorous Congress attackers. A vibrantly energetic man, he was able to save his skin and that of his colleagues too— sometimes suffering minimal injuries—because of his skills as a martial-arts expert. He also ended up being a target of attacks by individuals: in 1962, allegedly, a CPI member, Gangadara Marar, attacked him on the premises of the Thalassery court with a hammer, rendering him unconscious. (Marar was an eccentric who many years later apparently attacked the Muslim League leader C.H. Mohammed Koya with an acid bulb.)

Some people who had worked closely with Kurup, however, told me that when he was not backed by partymen, he was more tactful with forceful opponents. For instance, when the RSS pracharak V.P. Janardhanan, who was from Palakkad, sternly questioned him inside Kurup's own home (while the man was alone with his family) for destroying a photograph of Guruji Golwalkar from the venue of a proposed RSS function in Panoor, Kurup immediately apologized, sensing that Janardhanan would not budge for anything less. Many CPI(M) members too have similar stories to tell.

Incidentally, until its split, the communist party wasn't the invariably vindictive, overly spiteful entity it later became towards the opposition, especially in the Thalassery region, which would later become the epicentre of the political clashes in Kannur over the decades. Though there have often been cases of stand-offs between murderous Congress workers and the communists who were often at the receiving end as a party with inferior cadre strength, maintaining a perpetual combative posture had not been the case even in far more trying situations earlier. The only notable instance was when a few comrades, dressed up as cops, punched a Congressman named Vangana Kunhiraman in Dharmadam near Thalassery; the attack took place under the cover of darkness, and the man's nose was broken. That was in 1948.

The next such instance took place ten years later, when the undivided communist party's Pattiam Gopalan was beaten up by P.R. Kurup's PSP workers. Gopalan's friend and brotherly figure, Pattiam Kumaran Master, an educator and social worker, hired goons and dispatched them to Panoor to thrash the attackers in a tit-for-tat payback. But such incidents were an aberration rather than the rule, asserts former CPI(M) leader and educator Churayi Chandran. He believes that this sense of political propriety and their anti-violence stance were typically the hallmarks of communist leaders before the split. 'The culture of stabbing someone to death or settling scores like underworld mafia was not in practice before 1964,' avers Chandran whose study sessions for comrades in the 1970s and '80s were immensely popular.

Maybe its growing electoral prowess and the youthful leadership could have been the factors that forced the CPI(M) to think enough was enough. As MVR rose within the party, he institutionalized something that the CPI(M) had been cultivating since 1964: an extreme confrontationist stance. That perhaps was a result of its new-found influence among a larger section of people.

Chandran[4] feels that some CPI(M) leaders in Thalassery had a lot to do with ushering in this culture of targeted killings and an eye-for-an-eye approach, the most prominent being Arayakkandi Achuthan, who was a fiery orator, and part of a de facto 'ginger group' within the CPI(M) at that time. MVR, though he was not from Thalassery, was also part of this team, Chandran recalls. Several of these men took pride in roughing up political opponents. And in one instance in the mid-1960s, some RSS workers came under attack near the Valapattanam bridge. It was Arayakkandi Achuthan who led the charge while MVR too was part of it.

From 1971, MVR would face a new opponent as others faded away. N. Ramakrishnan grew within the Congress rapidly, becoming the state secretary of the Youth Congress in 1967 and then in 1971 the president of the district Congress committee (DCC) in Kannur when he was just thirty, eclipsing Gandhian leaders who were at the helm until then. A close associate of the Congress strongman K. Karunakaran—who was then the home minister of the state—Ramakrishnan was a rabble-rouser, an opponent who suited MVR's vendetta-driven, aggressive style of politics. *Kolavili* (war cry) is the term that journalists and political analysts have often used to describe this style of functioning. Both leaders fitted easily into their roles as perfect enemies, reinforcing the belief within either party that you ought to have one like them to take on the other. That they held their cadres under their spell added to the myth built around the two.

Ramakrishnan was seen as Karunakaran's prize catch to take on the worst enemy in its own den. MVR, for his part, was the cadres' cadre, a crowd-puller communist who mesmerized grass-roots party workers with his carefully modulated speeches, laced with earthy humour, slang, mild expletives, open challenges to the police and political rivals, and even sexual innuendoes. At a time when the Left leaders in the state were more obsessed with explaining their ideological standpoint, he had tailored for himself a more interactive style of oratory that immediately endeared him to the masses. He was blunt and crude when he launched into tirades against the party's opponents, especially K. Karunakaran, whom he allegedly referred to as '*Kallan* (Thief) or *Karinkali* (Traitor) Karunakaran'. And contrary to the plastic styles and angry tones of many of his peers, he was a communist who had trained himself to make people laugh. His sense of humour was infectious.

Ramakrishnan would remain the DCC president for eighteen years until he met his match in a politician of similar ilk: K. Sudhakaran, then a rising star in the Congress, beat him at his own game by securing a vote in his favour in the DCC elections in the late 1980s by use of force. Police reports say Sudhakaran had brought armed ruffians to the voting station in a DCC election to ensure a landslide win.

While Sudhakaran's ascent marked Ramakrishnan's steady decline in Congress politics, MVR would also face expulsion from his party in 1986, and the new party he floated, the Communist Marxist Party (CMP), soon joined the Congress-led UDF. Such was MVR's animosity towards the CPI(M) at the time of his exit from the party that—when called to the district committee office to explain his side of the story against the charge of indiscipline—he refused a cup of tea served to him, saying, 'How do I know this is not poisoned?'

Over time, MVR and Sudhakaran became thick friends in taking on the might of the Left, which had by then become the most formidable political entity in Kannur. Ramakrishnan, who had started off as a beedi worker and made his mark in politics through trade union work, was, of course, accommodated by his mentor, Karunakaran, in his Cabinet as labour minister from 1991–95. Karunakaran also found it useful to have a younger Sudhakaran to checkmate the Marxists in Kannur, though he had warned him not to go to excessive lengths to perpetuate violence. After Karunakaran's fall from grace in 1995 over the Indian Space Research Organization (ISRO) spy case,[5] which the Congress chief minister, ironically, had nothing to do with, Ramakrishnan, his acolyte, failed to make it to the top echelons of the state Congress. Ramakrishnan later had a brief tie-up with the Left—he contested the 1996 assembly elections with the support of the CPI(M) and other Left parties from the Kannur assembly seat, only to lose to Sudhakaran by a huge margin.

The 1990s saw massive confrontations between the CPI(M) and the Sudhakaran-led Congress, along with its new ally, MVR. From 1987–91, when the CPI(M) was in power, it had annexed the various enterprises in Kannur set up by MVR in the cooperative sector when he was a CPI(M) leader. The CPI(M) leaders had their reasoning behind this move—such institutions, including a hospital named after AKG, were built with the help of the party, with its members and sympathizers contributing their might to them. And MVR as leader of a single-member marginal party in the state assembly that survived on Congress's backing had no right over what was essentially a CPI(M) product.[6] MVR felt that he had the right over those cooperatives because his personal contribution to building them was singular. But the 'sweat equity' logic didn't have much appeal after the CPI(M) captured these institutions through elections and, according to reports from the time, even force.

When the Congress-led coalition won in 1991, MVR sought the cooperation portfolio from Chief Minister

Karunakaran, his former bête noire and now mentor, with a set agenda: to capture those lost cooperatives, especially the hospital, by all means.

What followed was turmoil, with even senior CPI(M) leaders being singled out for attacks, not to mention the numerous cadres who got hacked or shot down. The 1980s were turbulent, no doubt, with the cadres of the CPI(M) even being burnt to death inside their offices in at least one place, and Congress workers killed in retaliation; people were also killed in cases of mistaken identity, bringing to the fore the monstrous callousness of Kannur's killer squads and the scant importance they attached to a man's life.

According to the district crime records bureau, nineteen CPI(M) activists were killed in the 1980s compared to six from the Congress and one from the IUML. But the first half of the 1990s was worse, not specifically in terms of deaths but by way of maiming and the chaotic law-and-order situation. While fourteen CPI(M) cadres were killed, the number of Congressmen murdered was sixteen during the period of 1990–99.

In 1991, I stood near the Kannur railway station, waiting in anticipation for my mother to return after voting to elect the new panel of the AKG hospital. A professor of zoology at the prestigious Brennen College, and a government employee, she had bought shares in the hospital in the 1980s. I waited for her for hours; the routes to the polling station had been cordoned off by policemen who didn't allow me to go in. Three kilometres away from the polling booth, I was worried as rumours trickled down; one had it that even AKG's wife, Susheela Gopalan, had been harassed by the police and stopped from voting. It was also said that some CPI(M) leaders were hurt. MVR was paying back in kind the humiliation he had faced four years earlier when he had been forced out of the polling booth for an election to the panel of the same hospital and heckled out of his new office near Thekki Bazaar. As he walked back, a former comrade had offered him a garland of slippers.

The violence that day in 1991 went out of hand, with the CPI(M) using its organizational muscle to wreak havoc—and I saw it happen right before my eyes. Someone came to me to say that my mother would reach the railway station along with a cousin of hers on foot. I waited for a very long time until she finally arrived. We still had to walk back along the railway line that took us through winding routes and police barricades to get back home 7 kilometres away.

MVR won the battle for the AKG hospital, but not the war. Shortly, he would face disruptions from the CPI(M) wherever he went. His carcade would be stoned or stopped, or he had to face black flags.

And things took a really violent turn on 25 November 1994 in Koothuparamba where MVR arrived to attend a function, going against police advice. An irate crowd awaited him there. But, defiant like a street fighter, he goaded the police to shoot at his former comrades. Five Democratic Youth Federation of India (DYFI, the CPI(M)'s youth wing) workers were killed in the firing, earning MVR a bad name. That was only one of the many incidents when he used government machinery to his advantage in order to stop violent CPI(M) workers. When they provoked, he incited them back. Sometimes, he initiated it as though he enjoyed this wild political game. Such incidents also brought to light, once again, MVR's own role in promoting violence-laden politics. He and Sudhakaran were also accused of trying to kill a CPI(M) leader, E.P. Jayarajan, in 1995 on a train somewhere in Andhra Pradesh while he and others were returning from the CPI(M) party congress, the triennial highest conclave of the party, in Chandigarh.

Interestingly, in a disclosure to a TV channel, a former Congress councillor in the Kannur municipality, Prashanth Babu, who had also worked as a driver for Sudhakaran, said the leader had conspired to kill E.P. Jayarajan. He revealed that the conspiracy to eliminate Jayarajan had been hatched at Sudhakaran's house in Kannur's Nadal. Sudhakaran's associate and lawyer T.P. Hareendran (a leader of MVR's party) was also present at the house.[7] E.P. Jayarajan survived the attack, and the case against MVR and Sudhakaran (who allegedly used former RSS men to execute the crime) was later dismissed by the courts. Yet, an admission recently by

Sudhakaran about how MVR tried to protect him is damning. MVR apparently housed him in his official residence in Thiruvananthapuram while he was a minister in the UDF government, and lied to the Andhra Pradesh Police that he was not there. He also shouted at the special branch police officers who returned to his house at least twice. Later, MVR helped Sudhakaran shift to a safe location, the Congress leader confessed.

But the CPI(M) would soon override any threat from MVR or Sudhakaran. Both proved to be no match against Marxist militancy and resistance. On the contrary, the party would have a new foe, an entity it had been fighting for long, but one that would resurface with renewed vigour.

7

The Religion Card

The RSS and the undivided communist party had one thing in common: both faced bans, arrests and persecution in 1948. For the RSS, it followed the assassination of Mahatma Gandhi by Nathuram Godse, a former RSS worker. For the communists, it was the Calcutta Thesis of B.T. Ranadive that landed them in a soup.

At the time of its proscription, Kerala consisted of three regions: the British-ruled Malabar; and the two princely states of Kochi and Travancore. Kerala then had only twenty-one *shakha*s, the basic units of the organization, which typically meet daily.[1] Of these, four shakhas were in the undivided Kannur comprising the present-day Kasaragod district in the northernmost part. These four were in Kasaragod, Kanhangad, Kannur and Thalassery.

While the RSS faced an eighteen-month ban, the CPI was effectively banned from 1948–51 in all its major strongholds. Communist leaders later maintained that the 'Left-adventurist strategical-tactical and organizational line' adopted at the second congress of the CPI in 1948 was erroneous.[2]

Interestingly, in the Kerala region, hostilities between the Left and the right-wing RSS preceded this ban. While the undivided CPI was a well-knit organization, the RSS was in its infancy. Ranga Hari, one of the RSS's senior-most pracharaks in Kerala and a prolific writer, traces the roots of the conflict between the two entities to a day in early January of 1948, when young volunteers affiliated to the CPI barged into a public meeting of the then RSS chief Madhav Sadashiv 'Guruji' Golwalkar, shouting slogans to disrupt the function. Hari states[3] that the RSS youth retaliated suitably. Malayattoor Ramakrishnan, then a young pro-communist activist who later made his name as a bureaucrat and writer, was beaten up in the melee that followed. In his own inimitable sense of raw humour, he wrote later that the injuries from the thrashing healed, but the scars refused to go away, literally.

P. Parameswaran, a senior RSS pracharak and director of the Bharatiya Vichara Kendra, who has been conferred the second-highest civilian honour, Padma Vibhushan, has stated in a 2008 write-up that in 1949 too, 'there were two organized attacks, one at Kozhikode and the other at Alleppey [now Alappuzha] where Sri Guruji was addressing gatherings of Sangh Swayamsevaks . . . These attacks were pre-meditated and motivated by sheer intolerance and were totally unilateral.' The nonagenarian also added that in the 1950s when the RSS expanded its clout in the northern part of Kerala, including Kannur, the RSS pracharaks who went to work there were either threatened or socially boycotted, 'which included denial of boarding and lodging facilities. They had to take shelter in places like railway platforms.'[4]

While the communists faced the brunt of the Congress and government onslaught on its cadres, the RSS, which was a fledgling organization in what would soon be Kerala, found a new ruse to cope with the situation: setting up football, volleyball and basketball clubs, and organizing classes for the volunteers. It helped that the majority of its workers at the time were below the age of thirty.[5] As luck would have it, the Sangh could attract more young hires interested in physical activities to their fold. It thus found an opportunity in adversity through these months. The organization also took the young sevaks on short pleasure trips. During the period, the Sangh managed to get its new members from across Kerala to attend functions organized in Kaladi at the Advaita Ashram by Swami Agamananda, who had initiated the likes of P. Parameswaran into the Ramakrishna Mission.

For the CPI, large-scale reprisals across villages and towns strengthened the resolve of its supporters, who began to viscerally hate the ruling Congress party. Such utter contempt for Congress leaders whom they saw as malefactors transformed hundreds of villages, especially in the Malabar region, into communist strongholds. Literacy campaigns among women and the illiterate helped young people bond with the older guard who commanded their respect. The camaraderie was destined to last. Having been through the crucible of peasant and farmer movements, this was only to be expected.

While the communists were jailed in hordes, a few RSS pracharaks were also arrested and imprisoned. They included Dattaji Didolkar, who later became the RSS 'pranth pracharak' of Tamil Nadu; Shankar Shastri, the new pracharak in Malabar who replaced Dattopant Thengadi, who had been transferred to Bengal in 1944; P.K.M. Raja; Namadeva Kamath and Madhava Kamath. Others who had worked in Malabar such as T.N. Bharathan, P. Madhavan, R. Venugopal and T.N. Marthandan went underground.

The princely states of Kochi and Travancore adopted a softer stance towards the RSS and therefore the majority of those nabbed were from Malabar. But by the end of December 1948, sensing that the talks between Guruji Golwalkar—who was jailed following the crackdown on the RSS after the assassination of Mahatma Gandhi—and the government were going nowhere, the RSS began a nationwide satyagraha, and in

Kerala too, several people, including government officers, took part in the strike, and were suspended from their jobs. It was a crucial phase of growth for the RSS, whose activities in the state had been kicked off six years earlier by a Nagpur-based pracharak called Neelakanda Yashwant Telang, also known as Babu, who stayed in Thiruvananthapuram and made some contacts in the district and its neighbourhood for some six months. After him, Madhukar Krishna Oak was dispatched to Thiruvananthapuram, but he had to return in less than a year as he couldn't get used to the humid weather and local cuisine.

It was in 1944 that Manohar Dev, who was from Chandrapur in Maharashtra, came to Thiruvananthapuram as a pracharak; he stayed back for the next eleven years, setting the stage for the early growth of the RSS in South Kerala. But Ranga Hari notes that it was the Malabar division where Dattopant Thengadi influenced people to join the Sangh that ended up getting prominence over South Kerala in the RSS scheme of things. Thengadi was dynamic. He went to Thalassery in 1943 to initiate a few volunteers into the Sangh activities and, in no time, he was able to create a larger network in the area, especially among intellectuals, making things easier for Shankar Shastri to carry his work forward later. K.T. Chanthu Nambiar and P.K.M. Raja offered unstinted support to him in Thalassery.

Sajini, widow of the slain CPI(M) local leader C.V. Dhanaraj, with her sons, Vivekananda and Vidyananda, at their home in Kunnaru near Payyanur, Kannur. A music graduate, Sajini says she doesn't know whether she can ever get back to the normal rhythm of life.

A star-shaped photograph of CPI(M) activist Dhanaraj who was hacked to death outside his home.

The graveyard next to the Payyambalam beach, adjacent to which is a crematorium; the headstones here are those erected for communist icons A.K. Gopalan, Azhikodan Raghavan and N.C. Shekhar, among others.

Dipti Desai

Suchithra, widow of K. Mohanan, a CPI(M) local leader and toddy shop owner who was knifed to death by a six-member killer squad while he was at work in Valankichal near Koothuparamba, Kannur.

Dipti Desai

Kausalya, ageing mother of RSS leader K.T. Jayakrishnan Master who was hacked to death in front of his students in Mokeri Upper Primary School. She doesn't say a word to visitors at her home—her silence speaks louder.

Dipti Desai

A column built in memory of twenty-one-year-old ABVP leader Sachin Gopal in Payyambalam. He was killed by suspected members of the radical Islamist Campus Front, a feeder organization of the PFI. Police insiders say they even have teenage assailants on their radar

The signpost at Pinarayi village, the birthplace of Kerala chief minister and Marxist strongman Pinarayi Vijayan.

A memorial in Parappuram, Kannur, where the first Kerala unit of the Communist Party of India (CPI) was created secretly in December 1939.

A hammer and sickle, the communist symbol, in concrete at Muzhappilangad beach, Asia's biggest drive-in beach.

Brennen College in Thalassery, which has witnessed several violent clashes between ABVP and SFI activists. Former students of this institution include Pinarayi Vijayan, Congress leader K. Sudhakaran and BJP leader and lawmaker V. Muralidharan.

Pinarayi Vijayan with the late CPI(M) general secretary Harkishan Singh Surjeet. Chief Minister Vijayan, who is also Kerala's home minister, expects progress in the peace talks between the warring parties despite frequent relapses.

Courtesy of the likes of Thengadi, whose style of work is often compared to a tornado within the Sangh circles, Malabar became a prime spot for the RSS in the state. In 1947, at a major RSS camp held in Madras, the biggest units were from Madras and Malabar. For close to four decades, the RSS's activities in the state would be steered by Bhaskar Rao Kalambi, who was born in Dhansa, Maharashtra, and came to Kerala in 1946. He was the first 'pranth pracharak' of the state under whose watch the organization grew during its most turbulent years. He returned to Bombay in 1982 for advanced medical care.[6]

Political murders saw a spike following the Emergency, and transformed into a killing spree from 1979–80. Rao even believed he may have to face the murderous mobs himself. But both the Hindu nationalists and the communists avoided targeting the leaders on both sides to prevent the matter from snowballing into a national issue.[7]

The early pracharaks believed that it was not the RSS way to invite excessive attention to their work and sacrifices. The undivided CPI, which came to power through elections and created history in 1957, would return to power as the CPI(M) and the coalition leader in 1967, both times for two years. The CPI(M)-led Left Democratic Front (LDF) government came to power again in 1987, 1996, 2006 and in 2016. This time around, the man at the helm of the state, Pinarayi Vijayan, is someone the RSS loves to hate, and the feelings are mutual.

And in the meantime, the RSS's political arm, the BJP, has grown from being a minor player in central politics to the biggest party in the country, wielding power in twenty-one states either on its own or through alliance. The BJP has its chief ministers in seventeen of these twenty-one states, battering the grand old party, the Congress, which is in power in only four states as of mid-2018.

When I met J. Nandakumar in August 2017 inside a spartan room in a Lutyens' Delhi bungalow, he had just returned from the hospital. He had been unwell because of his habit of skipping meals. When he speaks, however, the grey-haired RSS pracharak is sharp, focused and unfaltering. His arguments about the frequent violence in Kannur—which has captured national attention thanks to the media, especially over the past decade—are compelling and original. While Nandakumar is looked up to by his RSS compatriots in Kerala as Nandettan the older brother, it is for the same reason that the CPI(M) sees him as dangerous, a Shylock of sorts who is seeking a pound of political flesh driven by vaulting ambitions. In person, he is the antithesis of his social-media avatar as a rabid anti-Marxist commentator. This senior leader of the RSS instead projects himself as a votary of peace, who wants to engage with the enemy to end the scourge of this mindless bloodbath. More importantly, he wants to put the spotlight on the vexing subject and would rather place things in perspective than sweep them all under the carpet. Whether or not he admits it, it is obvious that Nandakumar deserves most of the credit for transforming the Redtrocity campaign from an obscure internal awareness programme run by a handful of volunteers in Delhi into a countrywide blitz with participation from Hindutva leaders as well as the rank and file.

Nandakumar is national convener of the *prajna pravah*, which, for all practical purposes, is the intellectual wing of the RSS that steers several think tanks, and an all-India executive committee member of the organization, which, he says, is typically against any campaign targeting any particular party or individual. To buttress his claim, he invokes RSS's second chief, Golwalkar, who was once furious with a colleague for making an unsavoury comment about Jawaharlal Nehru's personal life and his habit of taking his daughter, Indira, on foreign tours. According to Nandakumar, Golwalkar stated in no uncertain terms to the crowd present there that it was unbecoming of the Sangh to cast personal aspersions on any leader, especially someone like the late prime minister, who had been a widower for long and therefore needed the help of his nearest family to support him in his advancing years.

Nandakumar argues that, for the same reason, it was with great trepidation—and only after all other options had been exhausted—that the Sangh decided to launch the Redtrocity campaign three years ago on a nationwide scale, following which the Kerala chief minister, Pinarayi Vijayan, faced public protests organized by the RSS on his visits to Delhi and Madhya Pradesh, where he was forced to skip a meet due to security reasons.

The rationale for the nationwide campaign highlighting the RSS as a victim and the dominant CPI(M) as a perpetrator was stark and simple—nowhere else in India does the RSS face such sustained challenges of physical elimination by its rivals, Nandakumar[8] emphasizes. Though the RSS has historically disfavoured such 'reactionary' propaganda, it had to do it as a last resort this time around, he avers.

To counter this charge, the CPI(M) has often stated that the RSS has found it easy to attack religious minorities and get away with impunity elsewhere in India, especially since the BJP government came to power at the Centre in 2014, but could not do so in Kerala due to the overwhelming presence of the Marxists who take a vow to uphold pluralism. Marxist leaders also bring up this obvious question: isn't the RSS actually targeting the CPI(M) in order to pull in votes from the Hindus who have traditionally favoured the Marxists in the southern state? The CPI(M) has always managed to secure a good chunk of the Hindu votes in Kerala, and the religious polarization that the RSS is known for has failed to click in the state so far. First, the CPI(M) won the goodwill of the powerful OBCs (other backward castes) mainly due to a series of legislations that benefited them following the successful redistribution of land by communist governments in the past. Second, a majority of its leaders until the 1990s were from the upper-caste Hindu fold, while its cadres were from the OBCs, and for decades the Left had distanced itself from any overt, official alliance with Muslim parties, sticking to Hindu voters as its mainstay. It is a different matter that Christians and Muslims in most pockets of Kerala typically favour the Congress not because the Marxists did not reach out to them enough, but because of the attitude of the churches and mosques towards communism, locally and globally.

Nandakumar laughs off the claim that the Marxists are up in arms against the RSS to save Muslims and other minorities from the Sangh. He sees a larger ideological scheming behind their motives to hobble the activities of the RSS from the very beginning. Why was Golwalkar attacked in Thiruvananthapuram as early as 1948, he asks. It was a time when communism was gaining momentum and it looked as if the globe was moving towards socialist rule. 'Why did a party with such a brute force in the state single out an organization like the RSS which was at an infant stage?' Nandakumar asks, suggesting an ideological divide, though perhaps it can just as well be a religious or moral one.

Nandakumar's Redtrocity initiative has been widely successful, especially outside Kerala, where, for Sangh workers,

Kannur has become a household name. Almost a microcosm of the macrocosm. On a visit to Sikkim and Assam in north-eastern India, I faced questions from conservative politicians about Kannur and its legacy of violence. Most of them would not be able to point out Kannur on a map, but the recall was immediate.

The leader tells me that the attacks and social boycott that the RSS has had to face, especially in the late 1960s and the 1970s, were a pan-Kerala phenomenon, to begin with. The killings and counter-killings between the RSS and the CPI(M) workers didn't occur in Kannur alone, he notes, saying that there were numerous skirmishes between the RSS and the CPI(M) in districts such as Palakkad, Alappuzha and Thiruvananthapuram. Though Vadikkal Ramakrishnan was killed in 1969 in Kannur, more RSS men were killed over the next few years, along with CPI(M) members, either in retaliation or in a premeditated fashion. Bhaktavalsalan, the 'mandal karyavah' of the RSS at Mullassery in the Chavakkad area of Thrissur, was killed in November 1973 and then reportedly dumped in a well. Veliyathunadu Chandrasekharan was killed in Ernakulam in 1970 and P.S. Sreedharan Nair in 1969 in Kottayam. Responding to these charges, the CPI(M) leader N.N. Krishnadas says he could reel off the names of the CPI(M) cadres slain by RSS men around the same period: T. Bhaskaran, CPI(M) worker and an employee at Victoria College, Palakkad, was killed by RSS workers on 3 March 1970; Syedali Kattapara, an SFI worker, was stabbed to death by RSS men inside Pattambi College in Malappuram in December 1974.

The list gets very long and the quibble longer.

However, if these inter-political clashes were a pan-Kerala phenomenon as Nandakumar puts it, why is it that Kannur alone gets a bad name?

Nandakumar says he had thought a lot about it. And for a long time, he had no answer. The obvious conclusion is that while in other places, including Alappuzha and Palakkad, where the RSS-versus-Marxists confrontations were rampant for some time, things are relatively back to normal now—and that is not the case with Kannur.

Nandakumar also feels that perhaps Kannur's notoriety has to do with the leaders at the helm of affairs—the likes of M.V. Raghavan, Pinarayi Vijayan, Kodiyeri Balakrishnan, E.P. Jayarajan, P. Sasi, P. Jayarajan, and so on—who have been vehemently disrespectful of rivals and their right to organize themselves. With the probable exception of a few CPI(M) leaders—like Sivankutty and G. Sudhakaran—the RSS leader says he has not come across leaders from Kerala's south, where he hails from, who espouse violence.

Without doubt, Kannur's Marxist leaders were (and some of them still are) vicious in their public denouncements of the RSS and other parties. Such lack of any modicum of respect for political opponents even on occasions of peace talks is proof of all that is wrong with the CPI(M)-dominated Kannur politics, Nandakumar says. MVR, in the 1980s, had reportedly shouted expletives at the RSS members at a peace meet organized by the district collector. In the bureaucrat's presence, MVR made a statement that has become part of Kannur's lore, something that even comrades of today repeat with a sense of pride: 'Stay away from us.' The CPI(M) leaders counter Nandakumar's allegations by saying that the RSS, too, is not far behind in verbal assaults, citing the speeches of leaders such as V. Sasidharan and Valsan Thillenkeri.[9] The latter famously said that the CPI(M) martyr U.K. Kunhiraman died not protecting Muslims from the RSS during the 1971–72 Thalassery riots, but in a drunken brawl in a toddy shop.

Nandakumar reckons that in places where the RSS had great sway from the 1960s to the '80s, it had never tried to clamp down on the communists the way the latter were doing to the Sangh workers in Kannur. Clearly, for the CPI(M), ideological hatred for the RSS runs deep, he says, dwelling at length on the violent disposition of some of Kannur's leaders who call the shots at the state level. He uses the word 'Kannurism' to describe their ideology as opposed to communism. At the same time, he disapproves of knee-jerk critics on both sides of the political divide who attribute the rise in violence to the RSS's arch-rival Pinarayi Vijayan becoming the chief minister.

'Both are wrong,' he says, adding that the RSS's decision to step up its campaign had to do with busting the myth about these confrontations. 'These clashes between the RSS and the CPI(M) are nothing new.' He pauses for a moment and then adds that Golwalkar is a godlike figure to people like him; he even cites the fact that Golwalkar had received initiation (*deeksha*) to sainthood in the Sri Ramakrishna–Vivekananda tradition. But the RSS chief had to renounce that route and plunge into social work. 'I have not been able to digest the politics of castigating such great men,' Nandakumar tells me.

Leftist historians and even police records offer a different picture of Golwalkar—that of a polarizer whom some CPI(M) leaders call an 'Indian Hitler' for what they consider his sour comments on other communities in his work, *We or Our Nationhood Defined*. At one of the Rajya Sabha sessions, the CPI(M) general secretary Sitaram Yechury had quoted some paragraphs from the book in response to a mention of the Third Reich by Finance Minister Arun Jaitley on 26 November 2015, drawing loud boos from the treasury benches.

Yechury quoted the following paragraph from the book published by Bharat Prakashan in 1939:[10]

... To keep up the purity of the nation and its culture, Germany shocked the world by her purging the country of Semitic races—the Jews. National pride at its highest has been manifested here. Germany has also shown how well-nigh impossible it is for races and cultures, having differences going to the root, to be assimilated into one united whole, a good lesson for us in Hindustan to learn and profit by.

In September 1978, Nandakumar, then just twelve years old, was deeply disturbed by the news of the murder of Panunda Chandran who was to attend an ABVP camp organized by the RSS. Nandakumar's brother Krishnakumar was slated to meet Chandran at the camp and there was a lot of discussion at home about the murder of Chandran, who was a young ABVP activist from a Marxist family hailing from the CPI(M) stronghold of Panunda in Kannur. Of course, within a month, on 26 October, there was a retaliatory strike on the CPI(M)'s Raju Master, his attackers slashing him to death.

Nandakumar is upset when journalists blame the RSS and the CPI(M) equally for the violence in the district. He contends that the CPI(M) has disagreements with 'everyone else' and not just the RSS. CPI(M) leaders such as P. Jayarajan respond to this by stating that the Congress and the RSS have often had secret electoral pacts and therefore had no reasons to 'quarrel'. This is not a mere allegation by a rival, but it's a publicly known 'secret' that the BJP has had vote-trade pacts with the Congress in the past. O.K. Vasu, who had left the BJP—first he floated a social organization and then went on to join the CPI(M)—tells me in an interview in December 2017 that when he contested the assembly polls as a BJP candidate in 1991, 'deals' were struck by the Congress with the RSS to transfer the latter's votes in the Peringalam constituency in Kannur.

Such a politically motivated nexus between the Congress, the Muslim League and the BJP—parties with supposedly opposing ideologies—was there for all to see in the Vadakara Parliament seat and the Beypore assembly constituency.[11] 'RSS votes shifted to the UDF's favour in as many as 50 Assembly constituencies, leading to an LDF defeat in 41 [seats],' reported *The Hindu* that year. The partnership was called *Ko–Lee–Bee Sakhyam* (a Malayalam acronym for Congress–League–BJP).

The only time the right wing and the CPI(M) were mildly sympathetic towards each another was during and in the immediate aftermath of the Emergency (1975–77) imposed by Indira Gandhi's Congress, which left cadres in both parties battered, physically and metaphorically.[12] In the 1977 assembly election, the BJS (predecessor to the BJP, founded in 1951 and dissolved in 1977) and the CPI(M) were said to have had an understanding in several seats, but that proved to be of no use to them. In Kerala, the alliance led by the CPI(M) performed poorly in contrast to national trends.[13]

Interestingly, the RSS had cleverly exploited the widespread anti-Congress sentiments during the Emergency to set up its shakhas in Marxist strongholds across Kerala, especially in Kannur. The organization ended up attracting many youths from CPI(M) families to its fold during the period, much to the anguish of the Marxists. The RSS cadres, including senior leaders, used their relative anonymity compared to CPI(M) leaders who were well-known faces, to organize such activities without attracting police attention. The Emergency was therefore a blessing in disguise for the RSS—their shakhas in Kannur grew manifold by the time the draconian law was lifted in 1977. Senior police officer Alexander Jacob has listed this phenomenon as one of the reasons for the conflicts between the two organizations over the next several years.

There is, of course, a twist in the tale. The Redtrocity campaign, which has evinced minimal interest within the state so far, has now launched a new fable that has become 'fast-food' for the so-called 'Internet Hindus' (RSS–BJP supporters and trolls online). As part of a larger game plan to woo Hindus towards the Sangh, it has been crying hoarse about a communist alliance with radical Islamists. While police records show no such unholy alliance, the rise of radicalized Islamist groups within Kerala—some of whose members have been found by the National Investigation Agency (NIA) to have travelled to the Middle East and Afghanistan, lured by the ISIS (Islamic State of Iraq and the Levant) call to wage jihad against the infidels—has nevertheless added spice to that tale (more in Chapter 8). Within Kerala, the Islamist PFI locks horns more with the CPI(M) than with the RSS, according to the police data available. Meanwhile, the RSS argues that the growth of pro-ISIS groups is due to the CPI(M) conniving with such outfits.

Founded in 2006 through a merger over the years of hard-line Islamic organizations such as the National Development Front, the Karnataka Forum for Dignity and the Manitha Neethi Pasarai of Tamil Nadu, the PFI also brought into its fold Goa's Citizen's Forum, the Community Social and Educational Society of Rajasthan, the Nagarik Adhikar Suraksha Samiti of West Bengal, Manipur's Lilong Social Forum and the Association of Social Justice of Andhra Pradesh. The organization earned itself notoriety, according to the federal agencies, for fomenting communal hatred and terrorism. As per these agencies, the organization wields influence among Muslims in twenty-three states and many more cities, and in the process, has spread its 'tentacles' at a fast clip in the past decade.

Ever since 2012 when former prime minister Manmohan Singh stated that Kerala—along with Jammu and Kashmir,

Assam and a few other states—had seen a spurt in religious extremism, the PFI had been on the Centre's radar, especially over allegedly masterminding a 2012 hate campaign against students from the north-eastern states who had to flee to their homes from boom towns such as Bengaluru and Pune in the face of online rumours of retaliation against them over attacks on Muslims in Assam. The PFI had denied any wrongdoing, but the NIA has recommended the ministry of home affairs to proscribe the PFI.[14]

Nandakumar is of the view that the threat is genuine. 'Pinarayi Vijayan shouldn't forget what happened to the pro-communist ruler in Afghanistan, Mohammad Najibullah, after the Taliban rose to the limelight,' he says with a smile.

He has reasons to smile. After all, the Redtrocity campaign has emerged as the most viable political tool for the right-wing ruling party at the Centre at a time when critics have found them guilty on many scores: majoritarian mob violence across many parts of India; attacks on Muslims and rationalists; abuses of power by the 'loony fringe', which has acquired mainstream presence; breakdown of law and order in states such as the BJP-ruled Rajasthan and Uttar Pradesh; a growing aggression towards freedom of expression in popular culture and arts, and so on.

Additionally, the RSS and the BJP are now making extra efforts to expand their influence in the south just as they did in new turf such as the North-east. And Kerala remains for them the final frontier to conquer. The RSS has set up more than 5600 shakhas in Kerala, more than it has in any other state.[15] Though the RSS had picked up in organizational strength in the state since the end of the Emergency in 1977, the BJP or its predecessor, the BJS, has had disproportionate electoral success. The BJP opened its account in the Kerala assembly for the first time only in 2016, winning one seat in the 140-member legislature. Senior BJP leader O. Rajagopal was elected from the Nemom constituency in Thiruvananthapuram district with a majority of 8671 votes, eating into the traditional Congress votes to batter his key opponent who belonged to the CPI(M).

Though the CPI(M)-led LDF cruised to a near two-third majority in 2016, the BJP saw its vote share rise significantly from 6 per cent in 2011 to more than 15 per cent. The party, which had aligned with the Bharath Dharma Jana Sena (BDJS) led by the Sree Narayana Dharma Paripalana Sangham general secretary, Vellappally Natesan, to pull in the numerically preponderant Ezhava votes, came second in seven assembly seats, much to the anguish of the Left and the Congress-led UDF.

As of now, outside the state, the RSS-steered media blitz has successfully managed to project workers of the Hindu nationalist party as more victims than perpetrators. The RSS and the BJP have also claimed that neither the Left nor the Congress, which have dominated political leadership in turns since the formation of the state in 1956, have protected the interests of the Hindus. The state is home to over 54 per cent Hindus; the rest are Muslims and Christians. The prosperity of the minorities in the state, many of whom have hit pay dirt thanks to the Gulf boom, has triggered much jealousy. Christians and Muslims also enjoy enormous political power. As of now, the CPI(M) wields tremendous clout among the Hindus of Kerala, which prides itself on its high social indicators.[16]

Amid the high-pitched blame game, Chief Minister Pinarayi Vijayan tells me in an interview in July 2017 that the RSS, with the exception of a handful of leaders, is not interested in any solution to the ongoing violence in the state, especially Kannur. A section of the RSS, which says it is the government of the day that has to take the initiative, feels that the chief minister's concerns, if any, are not shared by his comrades. As early as 2008, P. Parameswaran of the RSS had made the outline of his organization's demands in Kerala:[17]

It seems that there should be a three-point agenda which should be understood and accepted by all parties concerned, particularly by the CPI(M):

1. The CPI(M) should abandon the doctrine of 'Special Political Zone (SPZ)' sought to be imposed over Kannur district.

2. The CPI(M) should accept that the Sangh movement is an abiding reality in Kannur district as much as in any other part of the Indian Republic. This is a hard fact which cannot be wished away or denied by the practice of the philosophy of liquidation. Shakhas are an inalienable part of it.

3. They should give up the vicious belief that RSS-baiting, including politics of murder, can be a successful strategy to keep the minority community on their side in electoral politics.

The CPI(M), for its part, wants the RSS to shun its strategy of communal polarization and close down its arms-training centres.

Those are lofty goals to meet, and need personal and political will on both sides to even reach the negotiation table. But with the 'religion card' yielding political fruit for the RSS–BJP not just in Kerala, but also in its national agenda to alienate the leftists and win Hindu votes, and with cadres and hired guns aching to pounce on each other on both sides, peace in Kannur appears a distant dream.

8

The Anatomy of a Conflict

Two London-based friends surprised me a year ago with something I barely knew about Kannur when they said they wanted to visit a temple here to ride out the bad times in their businesses and personal lives. They didn't pronounce the name of the temple correctly, but when one of them typed it out as a WhatsApp text, I immediately thought of Alexander Jacob, one of Kerala's prominent police officers, now retired. Jacob has made a name for himself as a scholar of multiple religions, myths and legends about Kerala and elsewhere, and has an encyclopedic knowledge of Kannur and its history over centuries, besides that of world history. The sixty-three-year-old is a busy man these days, travelling about, giving speeches on Hinduism, Christianity and Islam at functions organized by a plethora of organizations cutting across caste and religious lines.

I had neither heard of Mridanga Saileswari temple located at Muzhakkunnu village in Kannur, nor even the legend that it was one of the 108 temples that the mythical Parashurama had consecrated in the state. The temple, I figured out later, had shot to fame after Jacob gave a talk about its idol of worship. The ornate Devi idol inside the temple had been carried away by thieves several times, but all such attempts had failed. Most thieves ended up defecating uncontrollably while carrying the idol, prompting them to flee in fear, abandoning the idol.

As a police officer posted in Kannur several times, Jacob knew the story of such cases of theft only too well. In his talk about the temple, he had also dwelt at length on how people who offered their prayers there were proved innocent despite serious charges of impropriety and corruption against them. They included senior politicians, police officers and non-Hindu artists.

Overnight, this obscure temple at a forlorn village in Kannur became a hub for pilgrims and tourists from all over the world.

As a person with great interest in supernatural events and social sciences, Jacob has done extensive studies over several years on Kannur and the propensity towards violence of an otherwise lovable population. Drawing materials from wherever he could, the former policeman has prepared an exhaustive report on Kannur's political violence and why it is a communal tinderbox ready to ignite. His findings make a mammoth manuscript running to 2000 pages. At the end of his Herculean effort, he handed over his work to the state police department from where, ironically, the work has gone missing, he says.

Luckily, he had preserved a personal copy.

Jacob, Kerala's former director general of police (DGP, prisons), has offered mainly eight theories for this phenomenon of cyclical violence in the region.

By attributing one of the key reasons to the 'martial nature of the people of Kannur', he has expanded on the notion that the Chekavar culture could be the root of the endless skirmishes. It is far more complex and deeper than it appears on the surface, he notes. 'People from this region have a different racial composition compared with people from other parts of Kerala,' he says.

A statement such as this could come under criticism from academics who usually rely on questions of social identity to arrive at conclusions about the bloodbath in this region. Whatever that may be, according to Jacob, the first known miscegenation (or what he terms the infusion of blood from warriors to the locals of the region that is now Kannur) was largely due to the Kolarians who lived along the coast of what is now Maharashtra and Gujarat. Their last king's name would be familiar to those who have read the Mahabharata: Kartavirya Arjuna, who had a thousand arms and was a powerful archer. Despite his muscular prowess and the military might of his kingdom, the king was killed in a fight with Parashurama, who, according to Brahminical myths, created Kerala by throwing his axe into the Arabian Sea. Brahmins, who formed a microscopic minority in Kerala, used this seemingly farcical theory as justification for their right over huge tracts of land in the region.

At the time of Kartavirya Arjuna's death, his last queen, Mahismati,[1] was in the advanced stages of pregnancy. Legend has it that she, in her last-ditch effort to give birth to a male scion, got on to a boat along with the slain king's followers and reached a place near where a naval academy now stands in Ezhimala (in Sanskrit and in the Mahabharata, it is referred to as Elisaila; *Kerala Mahatmyam* calls the hill Ezhimalai and Saptasaila; Marco Polo calls it D' Eli and Heili; Vasco da Gama's pilots in his ship also refer to the mountain that can be seen from far in the ocean). Here, she delivered a child who was named Ramakada Mushikan. The capital of his kingdom was called Ramanthali (in Payyanur) and his dynasty, Mushika, rose around the fifth or sixth century BCE. Ramakada was also called Iramkuda (from which the place, Eramam, in Kannur, gets its name).

According to Jacob's papers—which he painstakingly prepared after poring over volumes on ancient history, archaeological evidence and Sangam literature—there existed another famous Mushika king called Srikanta, who founded a city called Srikandapuram (now a town in Kannur). Another of their great kings was Vallabhan, who built a town called Vallabhapatanam, which later became Valapattanam (also in modern-day Kannur). One of their great kings who fought against the Chera (another dynasty in the south) army was Jayarajan (whose name is borne by three Marxist leaders—E.P. Jayarajan, P. Jayarajan and M.V. Jayarajan). The areas the Mushika kingdom controlled in the earlier stages and descriptions of their heroics come up very frequently in Sangam literature; in the Mahabharata too, there are references. Many of the royal families in Kerala trace their roots to this dynasty. According to historical documents, a treaty between the Cheras and the Mushikas was signed at a place near Narath (the home town of Congress leader A.P. Abdullakutty, who was earlier a CPI(M) lawmaker).

Nannan was another famous Mushika king, and a celebrated figure in Sangam literature. He had won many wars against other kingdoms, the most famous being the one at Pazhi (now called Pazhayangadi). Both Paranar, the court poet of Nannan, and the historian Atula have left notes about the various victories of the Mushikas. Eventually, however, more than 118 kings later, the Mushika kingdom passed on to the hands of the Cheras who at that time were led by

Narmudi Cheral. 'That [the coming of the Mushikas] was the first known infusion of "ferocious blood" among the people in the region,' Jacob posits. Mushikanagara (city of Mushikas) is described in an inscription (173–160 BCE) of King Kharavela of Kalinga in present-day Odisha.[2]

The second instance, he says, came with the advent of the 'Muthappan' culture: 'They say Muthappan [one of the deities earlier worshipped by the Buddhists who were marginalized by the Brahmins] came in a boat on the sea and reached Parassinikkadavu [which now houses a temple in his name and attracts lakhs of visitors].' Jacob sees Muthappan in conjunction with Porkali Bhagavathi (the presiding deity at a Kali temple in Kannur), who, he says, is actually a representation of the Assyrian goddess Nine (from which Nineveh, the Assyrian city of Upper Mesopotamia, located on the outskirts of Mosul in modern-day northern Iraq, got its name). The goddess is also called Astarte. A large section of the Assyrian army was battered by the Babylonians in the early seventh century, following which they escaped first into the sea. It is believed that their final destination ended up being Kannur (through sea and tortuous land routes). Muthappan, according to Jacob, has a resemblance with the Greek god Bacchus (later adopted by the Romans as their god of wine). Muthappan's favourite dishes are toddy and meat, and the devotees dutifully serve toddy as offering to Muthappan even today. 'That is how the Assyrian war culture came to Kannur,' Jacob tells me, rummaging through his voluminous work.

The 'third infusion of martial blood', according to Jacob, took place when the Kalabhras came to the region in the late seventh century. It is the only dynasty (which existed from the third to the seventh century) to have defeated the Cheras, Cholas, Pandyas and Pallavas. Their reign is referred to as the Dark Age in Tamil history, though their origin is unknown. Their most prominent king was Achuthavikandan who crossed the sea to what is now Lanka and brought in Buddhists from there. The Pandyas faced the brutally aggressive Kalabhras in a final battle in 680 CE and managed to defeat them, resulting in the loss of high status for the Buddhists. The Hindu religion thus became very dominant in the region that we now call Kerala, Jacob asserts.

Earlier, when Achuthavikandan conquered the Lankans, he brought the northern and eastern parts of that region under Kalabhra rule. Later, he recruited some warriors from there and brought them to Kerala; they joined the Kalabhra army and were called Chekavars, meaning fighters. That is why the Northern Ballads include this line: '*Njangalude poorvikar Izhathu nattinnu vannavarane.*' (Our ancestors came from Izham [Sri Lanka].) These people were also called *dweepan* (islanders); the word later became *Thiyyan* in Malabar (there is, of course, another theory that the Thiyyas came from Kyrgyzstan and yet another one that says they came from

Crete). Cyriac K. Pullapilly, a historian who was formerly an office-bearer at the Syro-Malabar Church, has written in a peer-reviewed journal that in North Malabar, there was a landowning dynasty of Thiyyas called Izhathu Mannanars who were Buddhists.[3]

After the Mushikas were 'subjugated', as stated earlier, they started training their children in kalaripayattu for the sole purpose of making them mercenaries. But being the marginalized community, they could only fight smaller duels over disputes between princclings or local chieftains (as explained earlier in Chapter 3). Each duel would first begin with a cockfight in which one cock would get killed. The king whose cock was killed could appeal, suggesting that humans fight to decide the final victory. 'The majority of the deaths even in the political violence of today are of the descendants of the Chekavars, the Thiyyas,' Jacob affirms, reeling off records. Professor T. Sasidharan, who has done extensive research on the subject, has also referred to this peculiar connection.

'So this racial mixing over centuries (Kolarians, Assyrians, Kalabhras and Lankans) is unique to the region that is now Kannur and not to any other part of Kerala,' Jacob offers, emphasizing that another round of miscegenation happened in the region with the arrival of the Portuguese.

The first time Vasco da Gama met Kolathiri (who ruled the region that is now Kannur), the North Kerala king found the Portuguese explorer munching nuts. When the king asked da Gama, who had landed in Kerala in 1498, to share the treat, the sailor offered a few pieces of what were actually cashew nuts. But, the legend says, Vasco da Gama refused to give the seeds of the cashew nut tree until the king gave him seeds of pepper in return. The king agreed. (Today, Kannur cashew is one of the biggest and the best varieties in the world.) Soon, the Portuguese began to settle in Malabar and Kochi, and since only men came on the ships, they mingled with the local women, especially those from Kannur. According to several historians and Jacob, the Portuguese preferred Nambiar and Thiyya women as partners. 'The Portuguese were a warrior race and this was a new "warrior blood infusion" into the area,' contends Jacob. (Dom Francisco de Almeida, the first Portuguese viceroy, built the St Angelo Fort on the western coast of Kannur in 1505; the Portuguese also built several churches in the district, one of which still attracts tourists.)

There had been one more stage of miscegenation earlier: it took place between the fourth and fifth centuries. During the time of the Kadamba dynasty (which ruled the Karnataka region), a Kshatriya clan shifted to Kerala. Many centuries later, in the eighteenth century, they formed the Pazhassi dynasty of Kottayam (in Kannur), covering what is today Thalassery taluk, Wayanad district, and Gudalur taluk of Nilgiris district. The Pazhassi kingdom had three branches: one headquartered in Pazhassi, now in Mattanur; the eastern branch near Peravoor (at Manatana); and another one near Koothuparamba. 'When [the Mysore king] Tipu Sultan invaded what is now northern Kerala, all others surrendered in the face of the brutal assault from his troops, but they [the Pazhassi king and his men] refused to do so. The British came later, and again, the Pazhassis refused to yield one inch; they kept fighting,' notes Jacob, referring to the wars at the end of the eighteenth and early nineteenth centuries.

The French came too. Bertrand-François Mahé of the French East India Company captured the area called Mahe in 1724, adding to the stream of racial intermingling in Kannur. Like the Portuguese, the French also came without their womenfolk, and married local women or kept them as concubines. Their influence spread in the Kadathanadu region, south of Kannur. Over and above all these, came the British. They forced the Portuguese to leave, but not the French from Mahe. They also had relations with local women. 'Such repeated racial mixing, especially with such martial classes, conquerors and explorers—all of them endowed with warrior-like qualities—is unique to Kannur, out of all of Kerala,' Jacob repeats. Kannur, which is often called the 'Crown of Kerala' and the 'City of Looms and Lore', was a major garrison town for the British until the late nineteenth century. According to British imperial records, together with

Tellicherry (now Thalassery), it was the third-largest city on the western coast of British India in the eighteenth century after Bombay and Karachi.

There were parallel cases of racial intermingling in the region when Malik bin Deenar and his troops arrived from Arabia in the eighth century. They married the native Hindu women and converted them to Islam. Incidentally, even Arakkal Bibi, who became part of Kannur's Arakkal Muslim dynasty, was originally from a Hindu royal family. The Arabs, who also contributed much to the racial resplendence of Kannur, were formidable fighters with extraordinary skills, wielding weapons like bows and arrows and various types of knives.

Academic historians and political scientists, however, disapprove of Jacob's style of analysis of the contemporary violence. Professor Nayanjot Lahiri, for instance, warns me that a hypothesis like Jacob's, which sees the roots of a current problem in remote antiquity, is implicitly stating that this is an intractable problem since this is innate and almost a part of the DNA of the region. According to Lahiri, an accomplished scholar and a historian of ancient India, 'What Jacob is saying is ahistorical, even as he cites myths and legends from the past, because history is based on a recognition of change.'

It took me many months to get an appointment with Alexander Jacob; he is forever busy giving talks on esoteric subjects as diverse as theology and the concept of Devi (Parvati). A few days before I met him, he had been in Kannur where he was the main speaker at a function organized by an ashram. On the evening of 4 February 2018, when I met him at his home near the famous Fatima College in Kollam, north of Thiruvananthapuram, he had come back from a similar function in Chengannur.

A bespectacled, tall and thickset man, he invited me to sit opposite him as he waded through the thick volumes he had prepared for the police department.

On the wall of his living room are photographs of Jesus Christ and Swathi Thirunal, the late raja of Travancore, who was also a brilliant music composer in both Carnatic and Hindustani styles. 'The next reason for Kannur's murderous politics is the composition of the population,' Jacob goes on, outlining his years of study of the subject which involved examining cases, crime data, folk tales, oral and written history in various languages, and the study of people, mythologies and legends.

In Thalassery, for instance, he says, Muslims still form the largest chunk of the population in the town and Hindus in the suburbs. 'This kind of ghettoization—natural or otherwise—is a real source for communal flare-ups,' he notes, referring to the riot that took place from late December 1971 to early January 1972.

In the Kannur 'city' area, which is around the old town and near the fishing harbour, Muslims are a majority, while the surrounding areas are thickly Hindu-populated. For instance, Valapattanam town is densely populated by Muslims, while Hindus are strong in the suburbs. 'Typically, in Kannur, the population of religious communities has been distributed in such a way that many places have become a powder keg for communal clashes,' says the bespectacled former police officer who is known for his calm disposition even in extremely tense situations.[4]

In the 1940s, when communism made its entry into the region, it mainly attracted people from communities such as the Ezhavas/Thiyyas and the Scheduled Castes in the region, while the top leaders were from the upper castes. The RSS at the time comprised mostly Brahmins and Nambiars/Nairs though they shortly began to make 'cosmetic' inroads into the coastal areas where the fisherfolk lived. The Sangh also recruited some OBC leaders into their fold to dispel the notion that theirs was an upper-caste–dominated entity in the district, just as it is elsewhere in India.

The Namboodiris and Nairs were a majority in and around the temple areas back then—and the trend continued for a long time. The Brahmins as well as the Nambiars mostly engaged in temple-related work, though professionals began to emerge from across communities who often remained apolitical.[5] At a distance from them lived the majority who were employed in beedi making, toddy tapping, and so on. This composition of the people made for a dangerous divide in the region, states Alexander Jacob, explaining that mixed communities are less likely to witness flare-ups.

The first major bout of violence triggered by this population distribution occurred on 28 December 1971, after members of a Hindu procession passing through a Muslim-dominated area of Thalassery town allegedly attacked some Muslim boys. Police records show that things precipitated after an incident near a hotel named Noorjehan. There are several 'popular' versions of the incident. One has it that two Muslim youths were fighting inside the hotel and one of them hurled a slipper at the other; when he ducked, it landed on a member of the procession on its way to a temple nearby. There is another version that the slipper flew through a window of the hotel and landed exactly on the idol that was being carried to the temple. The RSS's version is that it was a deliberate act—and that it couldn't be divine intervention that the slipper accidentally landed on the idol—by the Muslims to provoke the Hindus into a riot.

The Hindu marchers soon entered the hotel and went on a rampage of destruction. As rumours spread, Muslim groups retaliated the next day. What followed was utter chaos: even some of the Marxist beedi workers who were Hindus (and whom I spoke to) were agitated to hear what later turned out to be wild rumours—that young Hindu women were stripped and that murderous mobs of Muslims chopped off the breasts of some Hindu women heading to the Jagannatha temple, set up by the great reformer Sree Narayana Guru. It is a temple frequented by people from all Hindu groups, unlike the Thiruvangad temple in Thalassery, which was once a preserve of the upper classes. The idea of spreading such rumours was to generate resentment among a large section of Hindus. P. Jayarajan of the CPI(M), who was a young man then and was at the scene of the wanton destruction of property, argues that if such rumours had been linked to the Thiruvangad temple, fewer people would have turned up.

Thalassery, incidentally, had had a history of communal riots that mostly involved looting and setting fire to the shops of rival communities. Such incidents had been reported in 1934, 1937, 1940, 1946 and 1948. On most occasions, the fight was between the Thiyyas and Muslims, many of whom were attracted to the idea of the two-nation theory before Partition. Abdul Sather Sait, a Muslim League leader from Thalassery, migrated to Pakistan upon its formation and later became a diplomat in that country.

Pattiam Rajan heard the news of the arson and rioting in Thalassery on the morning of 29 December at eight o'clock when he had reached the Koothuparamba court. He wasn't a full-timer in the CPI(M) yet, and had a flourishing practice as a lawyer at the time alongside his role as a party leader. He immediately hired a vehicle and in the company of fellow comrades K.V. Vasu and P. Jayarajan headed to Pinarayi to fetch Pinarayi Vijayan who was recovering from a viral fever. Vijayan remembers that morning vividly: 'I had come out from home since I was feeling better and was having tea [a habit he says he stopped a little while later] at a local shop when Rajan and others reached the spot. They broke the news of the riots that had started off in and around Thalassery following some clashes the previous day.'

Immediately, Vijayan popped some fever pills and they all headed to the Thalassery office of the CPI(M) via Kolasseri, and contacted the leaders who were away for a state committee meet. Before the likes of senior leaders C.H. Kanaran, M.V. Raghavan, Pattiam Gopalan, O. Bharathan and others arrived after the meeting from Thiruvananthapuram, the young comrades were asked to install a CPI(M) flag in front of their vehicle and drive across the affected part of the town appealing for calm. And while they were doing so, a CPI(M) sympathizer asked the young leaders whether there was any Muslim inside their vehicle—though the CPI(M) members and affiliates were trained to be secular, there were many who got swayed by the passions of the moment and turned communal. Pattiam Rajan remembers Pinarayi Vijayan silencing the man with his combative replies. 'It was our youthful vigour to brave any odds and even to sacrifice ourselves that guided us all through the drive, which turned dangerous at various moments,' recalls Vijayan.[6] The appeal for calm and the stern demeanour of these young leaders gave the Muslims a palpable feeling of safety: that the Marxists were with them. It also dissuaded the Hindu attackers, who sensed that the organizational machinery of the CPI(M) that had shown an olive branch now would not hesitate to come back with vehemence if anyone dared obstruct them. The Justice Vithayathil Commission Report would later commend the CPI(M) cadres for their efforts to quell the violence.

AKG, who was unwell at the time, didn't immediately head to the scene of the riots though he was aching to go. EMS dissuaded him from going and chose to go himself to appeal for calm. By the time AKG arrived later, normality had been restored in the town. A political commentator and veteran journalist formerly associated with the *Deshabhimani* had accompanied both EMS and AKG on their visits to the trouble-prone areas of the town. I.V. Shivaraman—who, too, had reached the spot along with the likes of CPI(M) leader E.P. Krishnan Nambiar on 29 December, a day after the riots— remembers EMS, on 30 December, pleading with the rioters to end the violence at his leader's (AKG's) behest. It worked.

However, RSS leaders argue that the rioters were all CPI(M) men, which was why they dispersed when asked to by the Marxist leaders. They argue that it was the CPI(M) members themselves who had triggered the attacks on Muslim shops and houses. RSS leader Valsan Thillenkeri[7] has made several speeches accusing the CPI(M) of indulging in violence. However, the fact that the Muslims of Thalassery stood solidly behind the CPI(M), especially in all elections since then, is proof of what the truth could be.

Alexander Jacob, for his part, laughs off the RSS suggestion. He quotes police records, which concluded that the CPI(M)'s effort was to protect the Muslims who were being targeted.

More than 400 shops were gutted and 250 buildings were ransacked during the Thalassery riots,[8] but not a single rape was reported. In Kerala, women are always spared, if not respected, even during riots. Neither were there any deaths— just as there were hardly any deaths in similar riots in the rest of Kerala. Deaths from riots have been reported only since the mid-1990s, points out Alexander Jacob.

In Thalassery, the idea was to destroy the trade infrastructure of the Muslims. The CPI(M) admitted later that the anti-Muslim League tirade by the party after the fall of the EMS government when the Muslim League withdrew support—and joined hands with the Congress and the CPI— had, of course, created an anti-Muslim feeling among the party cadres. AKG had led a jeep march from Kasaragod to Thiruvananthapuram campaigning against the League and its 'double standards'. With such a respected leader hitting out at the League, the sentiment among the Hindus, especially in Thalassery, known for its Hindu–Muslim business rivalry and having seen communal skirmishes in the past, was vehemently along religious lines. Besides, the decision of the Muslim League to celebrate fifty years of the Malabar (Moplah) Rebellion, which many historians and Hindutva politicians believe was an anti-Hindu massacre, also ruffled feathers.[9]

After the riots were contained, the Marxists dismissed those party members who had got carried away and taken part in the violence. The RSS was clever enough to tap into the opportunity and lure them into their own organization. The Hindutva organization gained more cadres as more riots, smaller ones, took place in the region, while the CPI(M) won the Muslim vote bank in Thalassery.

But the truth is never as simple as it seems on the surface.

The police administration reports on the 1971 riots that I accessed state that on 28 December, around 11 a.m., a religious procession started from Eranholi via Thalassery overbridge heading to Meloottu Madappura (dedicated to Lord Muthappan). As many as 300 people were part of it and most of them were drunk. 'The marchers had excessively imbibed the toddy that they had collected as an offering for Muthappan,' says the report (loosely translated from Malayalam). It goes on to say that some of the inebriated marchers provoked the crowds in the city by first beating up two Muslim boys. They also stopped autorickshaws as they walked past, in an apparent show of Dutch courage and mob mentality. When the procession reached Noorjehan Hotel, an irate young Muslim boy hurled a slipper at them. Though most members ignored it and walked away, those at the rear end barged into the hotel and beat up the hotel owner, Hamsa, and his apprentices. Following this, some of them threw stones at the madrasa and the mosque in Narangapuram, while some others walked into the mosque and beat up a person named Usman who was asleep inside. Later, they began to attack Muslim homes and shops. They also attacked a mosque in Ayyaneth.

According to the report, the Muslims began to hit back on 29 December, first near the Saidarpalli and Mattambaram mosques where Hindu shops came under attack.

The Marxists see it as an irony that CPI leaders (who were in power at the time) accused the CPI(M) of being participants in the riots. The police reports—of a government led by a CPI chief minister—and the inquiry commission that followed both lay the blame for the riots on fundamentalist forces in which both Muslims and Hindus suffered huge losses. The CPI(M), on its part, accuses the RSS of orchestrating the riots and the Congress–CPI government of the day of conniving with them.

Over the past few years, news reports have appeared suggesting a 'huge role' played by the current national security adviser (NSA), Ajit Doval,[10] an IPS officer in the Kerala cadre, in containing the riots while he was dispatched there by the then state home minister K. Karunakaran for a brief period from 2 January to 9 June 1972. Pulikkodan Narayanan, the then subinspector of Kannur town who later became a henchman of Karunakaran during the Emergency, has said that Doval did a good job, especially in retrieving looted property. Doval was then an assistant superintendent of police (ASP) in Kottayam district. The CPI(M)'s P. Jayarajan isn't pleased by this proclamation at all: he describes it as a new 'myth-making' exercise.

Meanwhile, Churayi Chandran, former CPI(M) leader, says he has never been able to really fathom the undercurrents of the Thalassery violence. 'I am still confused about what contributed to the incident,' he tells me in an interview, leaving room for further blame games.

Within a few years after the Emergency, the RSS, emboldened by roping in cadres from the CPI(M) into its own fold, launched several attacks on Dinesh Beedi companies, bastions of the CPI(M). By late 1979, the CPI(M) realized that the party was under attack within its own den. The Marxist retaliation was brutal. For every Marxist who was killed, three RSS men[11] had to die, the party decided. 'M.V. Raghavan was then the *mudichooda mannan* [uncrowned king] of Kannur,' remembers Jacob.

MVR had by then groomed several leaders who could be as abrasive as he was, although there were ups and downs in his relations with them: Pinarayi Vijayan, Raju Master, Kodiyeri Balakrishnan, E.P. Jayarajan, and so on. 'The grace of AKG in times of skirmishes disappeared when the mantle fell on MVR,' notes Jacob. 'From resistance, it became sheer violence.'

The third theory of Jacob's has to do with geography and weather.

He writes in his manuscript:

The geography of Tellicherry [now Thalassery] is conducive for riots. The sea coast and the Eranholi River, which flows through the centre of Tellicherry town, facilitate the influx and escape of anti-social elements, including rowdies and goondas from nearby areas, the slum areas of Thalai, Chalil, Mattambram, Saidarpalli, et cetera, with narrow lanes and unapproachable areas that are the breeding grounds of violence. These areas also make it difficult for the police to operate. The town is something like a triangular projection into the sea, which is also a factor that helps rioters.

The ease with which a rioter can escape is a crucial factor, and this makes the police's job tougher, he rues, adding that he was encouraged to take up this study by his senior colleague Arvind Rajan in 1985 when both were discussing the gruesome crimes in Kannur.

Earlier, crime followed a cyclical pattern, explains Jacob. In the 1980s, it would start around 15 October, peak by December and peter out by March. After the reaping season of October, the farmer was relatively free and essentially unemployed for the next three or four months. 'Such people can easily be lured with money. Though I haven't heard of the CPI(M) having to bribe youths to do their bidding, other parties routinely did it. Both the Congress and the RSS used to do it,' Jacob states.[12] Cat-calling, or harassment of women, by such dawdling men also led to clashes. And after the summer rains of March, all would go back to the fields and have no time for criminal activities.

Jacob has tracked vendetta crimes of almost 500 years, collecting data from British and earlier archives. The data is stunning: 80 per cent of such crimes took place from October to March.

Now, with people opting for tertiary-sector jobs, the trend is changing, but what contributes to the incidence of crime is, still, unemployment. As Sasidharan and others have pointed out, it is the lower classes that fall for the trap of political parties which offer them a certain new identity and recognition in exchange for engaging in partisan violence.

Scholars have noted that due to the abysmal factory output and therefore jobs, especially in North Malabar, the brightest ones enter government or highly paid private-sector jobs. The rest mostly manage to secure jobs in the Gulf region and send back money, which triggers a competitive consumerist culture; flashy cars, luxury homes and high consumption of everything from fancy gadgets to exotic food products are reflective of this trend. Those who get left out either do odd jobs and stay content, or become cannon fodder in the competitive and violent politics of the districts.

A random analysis of the leaders of the killer squads of the CPI(M), the Congress and the BJP–RSS over the past twenty years with the help of a police officer who wants to remain anonymous reveals that not even 1 per cent of them make it to leadership positions. They are often made to feel important by their leaders who support their families in times of crises, which include imprisonment or threats from rivals. In the prime of their youth, they are offered money and perks, but gradually, they are sidelined based on their crime records and the public perception that they are gang leaders who assist their party in carrying out attacks on rivals.

In the case of the RSS, the sample was limited because a good majority of them were recruited from elsewhere, leaving no trace of where they came from. Yet, the perception is that the pracharaks—the new ones—who come from elsewhere have no commitment to the places where they are briefly based and therefore act most indiscriminately in promoting violence. O.K. Vasu and A. Ashokan, both of whom were targets of bomb attacks after they left the BJP to join the CPI(M), state openly that the RSS pracharaks from elsewhere these days are an irresponsible lot. Ashokan,[13] while he was with the RSS–BJP, had to thrash a pracharak named Pavithran who had come to his locality and ordered that the CPI(M) workers be killed in retaliation for some violence far away, he says.

O.K. Vasu alleges that a very senior leader of the RSS from Kathiroor was directly involved in the killing of Raju Master in Panoor in the late 1970s. Sashidharan, a key accused in the attempt to murder P. Jayarajan and a witness in the Kathiroor Manoj murder case, has been allotted five Central Reserve Police Force (CRPF) officers for his protection. It's another matter that the RSS leaders accuse even topmost CPI(M) leaders of having a criminal past.

Mostly, however, the ringleaders of the killer squads are often left on the fringes once their utility expires. As of now, the Puthankandam brothers—Premjith and Pranoob—call the shots in the RSS near Venduttai under the Kathiroor Police limits. This gang is collectively called the 'Venduttai set'.[14] The police had some years ago recovered thirty-six bombs near their residence—of the thirty-six, thirty-five were powerful steel bombs and one was an 'ice cream bomb', all of which were found abandoned in a vacant plot when a raid was conducted based on a tip-off.[15] The police say the RSS has introduced new weapons and modus operandi of attacks, including the use of bombs in Kannur. Initially, they had burst fireworks used in temples and celebrations as tools to launch their strikes.

But the aspirations of the gangsters to make it to the upper echelons of political power tend to go awry. Those who take part in direct violence are mostly fated to stay at the bottom or the middle of the ladder; these members are easy to discard whenever they display some ambition. There are occasions when party leaders across political lines take undue advantage of their loyalty. Allegedly, the RSS didn't even bother to collect the body of one Haridasan (originally from Atholi in Kozhikode) who had supposedly gone to Pattiam in Kannur to launch an attack on a beedi company, and got himself killed. Others who were part of his team ran away to the safety of an 'RSS village', Kongachi, but as a stranger to the place, he was at his wits' end after having exhausted his bombs, which he had hurled at the beedi-making shops. Cornered from all sides, he was stoned to death by an angry mob.

Some others tend to be luckier if they can diversify and start from scratch. Allegedly, K. Janardhanan[16] of Thazhe Chovva had been the mastermind behind the targeted murders of political rivals for decades. So goes the popular perception, which he neither confirms nor denies. He just tells you sincerely that he doesn't want to talk about the issue of political violence in Kannur. In all probability, he holds numerous secrets and is perhaps a cadre from a generation taught to keep secrets secret. Groups of young men now look up to the former beedi worker for his meticulous planning and secretive ways—but back in the 1980s and '90s, not many people bothered even if they knew who killed and who didn't. Political violence was seen as a daily affair although its vilest heights were yet to be achieved.

The common man didn't know much about the police action that followed each murder, but party workers were arrested and some convicted and sent to jail. After every attack on political rivals, the accused political parties voluntarily offered the police a list of perpetrators from their side. The police then arrested those persons. Like many others, Janardhanan himself had been on such lists and had spent time in jail. Over time, he began to command more respect from his violent followers than the leaders he reported to. He was charming in his own way and his sidekicks worshipped him. Party workers still often drop in to his office where he now practises *marma chikilsa* (a healing regime that focuses on applying pressure on the sensory parts).

In his heyday, Janardhanan knew how to melt easily into a crowd. He had a pleasing disposition, and was never the muscle-flexing bully who stood out. He didn't look like the kalaripayattu exponent that he was, a man who knew how to wring someone's arm and lock it in a way only he could unlock. He was capable of immobilizing people by placing his fingers on the marmas, the sensory points in the body. Clearly, they don't make the likes of him these days; he is unassuming even by communist standards. Most of the new cadres, trained to 'resist' the so-called onslaught against the party and to physically eliminate enemies, have piercing eyes, sobered only by alcohol or excessive tobacco consumption. Some of them are gangsters who are loyal to the party that feeds them, but they are not party loyalists. Janardhanan, on the other hand, is old school, a neighbourhood uncle by appearance, his smile eternally innocent due to the childlike crinkle of his eyes and the glitter of healthy, well-lined teeth, his voice gentle and his demeanour that of a householder going about his tasks. Unlike those bragging hitmen who use their proximity to political parties for personal gains and money, in Kannur and elsewhere in Kerala, Janardhanan is a puritanical party worker who for a long time placed the party's interests above his. The most remarkable thing about such commitment is that you don't let any sense of morality clutter your action. In his prime, he was apparently someone who could accomplish his mission, return to eat a hearty dinner and then sleep like a baby.

Clearly, behind this avuncular, cheerful persona of a long-time survivor of a series of attacks by political opponents and killer squads is a Marxist idealist who is thoroughly convinced that his party, the CPI(M), has to obliterate opponents who make lives miserable for its comrades. For him, violence isn't a vulgar indulgence, but a necessary resistance to quell the hardship of party members under constant attacks from goons of other parties. As recently as 2009, he had suspected that a gang of hired guns who had arrived in Kannur reportedly to bump off a CPI(M) rebel and now Congress legislator was actually sent by the son of one of his alleged victims in order to finish him off. But it was a botched attempt. Several members of the RSS killer squads disclose in whispers that Janardhanan has escaped death by a whisker several times over the past two decades. Garrulous Congressmen too make such claims.

Janardhanan doesn't justify any kind of violence that he feels is not absolutely imperative. Until the early 1970s, Marxist comrades couldn't enter many parts of Kannur—including his current turf, Thazhe Chovva, which translates as Lower Mars—without getting beaten up, allegedly, by Congress workers. Janardhanan discloses to me that the Congress assailants, who were often patronized by the police, routinely targeted the workers of the undivided CPI. It was against this 'injustice' that force and violence had to be used, he reasons. As tensions mounted, clashes continued in the 1980s too. In 1985, a noted Congress local leader, Puthiyandi Bharathan, and his men allegedly stabbed O.P. Krishnan, a CPI(M) worker, very badly. The Congress was in power, but the local workers of the CPI(M), as the rumour goes, didn't want the act to go unpunished. So, say the police records, the comrades attacked Bharathan who then bled to death. This set the stage for a large-scale mobilization of forces between the Congress and the CPI(M), resulting in almost two decades of skirmishes and numerous deaths in that part of Kannur.

Janardhanan is an *abhyasi* (one well versed in kalaripayattu) who started practising kalari from early childhood. The teetotaller and frugal eater retains a healthy physique. An apocryphal story goes that when he was sent to a physical training camp organized for select party members, the master of the course found that he had nothing to teach him and so named him the trainer instead, especially when it came to marma techniques and hand-to-hand combat, knife and sword fights. Various party members have, over time, approached him for learning such skills and he has obliged them. He earned a league of disciples not just for his martial skills but also reportedly for the great care he always took in ensuring their safety during any 'operation', a code name for violent strikes on adversaries.

Janardhanan's office, filled with numerous herbal potions and traditional oils, isn't very easy to spot. One has to take a stairway from behind a building in Thazhe Chovva, a small town which has now become a CPI(M) bastion after being a Congress stronghold until three decades ago. According to CPI(M) lore, when the late CPI(M) leaders R. Krishnan and a few others once held a meeting in Chovva in the late 1960s, they were showered with the choicest abuses by the local Congress toughie C.T. Lakshmanan who used to run a cycle shop around there. Nobody could do anything to stop his drunken revelry against their respected leaders. That is now a story the local Marxists recall with regret and a sense of shame.

Janardhanan was one of the prominent party henchmen who worked hard, and I had watched him emerge as a symbol of the CPI(M)'s muscular prowess in the area. From the early 1980s to 2005, he is widely believed to have played a pivotal role as a key behind-the-scenes operative for myriad acts of eliminations of the party's detractors across the district. While he was busy battling the Congress party in the central and northern areas of this politically volatile region, he also had a huge role to play in assisting the local leaders in the southern parts obliterate RSS antagonists, especially in places that have now made national headlines: Thalassery and Panoor.

As a boy, Janardhanan frequented kalaris not only to learn the martial art but also to master the traditional medical system practised by the kalari masters, mostly for treating bruises, whiplashes, sagging, muscle injuries, fractures, and so on. He had also made tours to forests in search of herbs to make medicines. His father had been a beedi worker, and Janardhanan had followed in his footsteps. Fifty-two years ago, he occupied the rooms he now uses for his healing work. 'The rooms in this office have changed a little bit, but this is the same space,' he says.

Janardhanan, according to the CPI(M) leaders I spoke to in Kannur, was castigated in 1994 for getting a party worker thrashed for claiming in a closed-door meeting attended by several delegates that the slain SFI leader K.V. Sudheesh was a victim of revenge killing after Janardhanan's squad sliced the legs of RSS pracharak Sadanandan Master around his knees. He then spent time in jail over murder charges and faced disciplinary action from the CPI(M) reportedly over some of his men killing an innocent man in Koodali, 15 kilometres south of Kannur town, in 2005.

But he has nothing against the CPI(M), he insists softly, emphasizing that he is in touch with the district leadership of the party. After all, it was apparently the party that relocated him to the Middle East when the police and rival Congressmen launched a manhunt against him over a case involving the death of a Congress worker in the 1990s. Yet, his loyalists confide in me that 'Januettan' isn't mightily pleased with criminals taking over the reins of the party and wreaking havoc by targeting innocents and perpetrating crimes even against those who did not harm the party members. A section of CPI(M) leaders, meanwhile, accuses several men close to Janardhanan of working like 'quotation gangs', a term for hired guns who kill for a fee.

For a man whose image has been deeply besmirched as the brain behind numerous murderous acts against rival party workers across the district, for training scores of men to make country bombs and to carry out perfect murders using sharp weapons, Janardhanan is a contradiction. He is said to have warned the party leaders against the 'injudicious' use of the party machinery to execute personal grudges. (Some of those leaders include people who have cultivated an image of being peaceniks.)

Janardhanan stops talking when asked about how the cadres are prepared for operations, after mildly suggesting, 'I can't speak because I can't lie to you.'

The party idealist has patients waiting for him. Meanwhile, he tells me that the brutal murder in 2012 of T.P. Chandrasekharan, a CPI(M) rebel who floated a new outfit, the Revolutionary Marxist Party (RMP) in 2009, in neighbouring Kozhikode district was unwarranted. He has no sympathies for the breakaway group, but he feels that the takeaway from the heinous murder (Chandrasekharan had fifty-one knife cuts on him) is that the party leaders were caught off guard when the police arrested the real culprits and obtained call-record data of the key operative who probably steered the attack, P.K. Kunhanandan, a CPI(M) member. It is very likely that the call records contained numbers of party leaders whom Kunhanandan had interacted with. The widely circulated story is that before the killing, even the gangsters[17] could foresee that the murder would throw things out of gear for the CPI(M). In fact, one of them is said to have asked whether he should abort the bid. Kunhanandan reportedly snapped at him, perhaps in a spurt of overconfidence that the probe wouldn't reach him, and ordered him to just carry on and do his job.

In Janardhanan's time, the police accepted the names of the people listed out by each party, be it the CPI(M), the Congress or the RSS–BJP, as those who took part in a crime. Often, the undertrials were innocent and had to be released for lack of proof. But now, such convenient 'owning-up' is history due to CCTVs, call records and other advances in technology.

Januettan's patients get impatient as we speak, but the man will not ask a visitor to leave. Such courtesy is typical of the people of this stunningly beautiful coastal district known for its breathtaking beaches, hills and warm-hearted people. For a moment, one is left to rue the intellectual bankruptcy of the leadership that shoves a loyal cadre into savage acts long after the age of resistance against oppressive witch-hunts was over. It is a different story that in Kannur, Janardhanan has his counterparts in the RSS and the Congress too.

Wayanadan Thamban, the nom de plume of one Ayyappan of the RSS who has unleashed violent tactics in various parts of Kerala against the Marxists, especially in the 1980s, remains a recluse. The mystery about him adds to his mystique as a gruesome killer with astonishing martial-arts skills and dexterity to flee to safety from knife-wielding assassins and mobs. He was reportedly killed in 1986, but police suspect it was a case of mistaken identity and that the celebrated RSS mercenary is still alive and kicking.

And behind such tales of valour and brutality lies the naked truth: the lower rank and file always tend to pay a heavier price for political immaturity, as is evident from the RSS–CPI(M) clashes of the 1980s in Thalassery when there would be an abrupt ceasefire at the slightest hint that the leaders of both parties, and not ordinary workers, would become the next targets.

Notably, former hitmen live miserable lives after their prime—and perhaps die of guilt.

The inadequacy of police action is another major Achilles heel for Kannur. For almost 30 lakh people, there are just over 3000 policemen in the district notorious for its cyclical violence. So is the paucity of police vehicles, say the officers posted in the district. The absence of a comprehensive riot-tackling scheme—though one has supposedly been in place since the late 1990s—continues to be a cause for worry, says Jacob.

Jacob concedes that policemen—including those under his command—used to accept the list offered by the accused party, primarily because they lacked the wherewithal to investigate and trace the real culprits in most cases. He remembers that in the Edakkad police station, one of the subinspectors had given him a list of the accused, which carried the name of one who was already dead. 'Such was the nature of investigation,' he says, adding that in the T.P. Chandrasekharan murder case, the police refused to accept the list offered by the accused party, the CPI(M).

These days, though, the deputy superintendent of police (DSP) P. Sadanandan of Kannur says that the police tend to accept the list given by the victim's party, who often name big leaders with the hope of making the case 'stronger'.

Though the police are more or less prepared to prevent revenge murders, it is the orchestrated nature and the meticulous planning behind the attacks by the communal outfits that are a major menace in Kannur, says Jacob. 'Organizations such as the RSS, PFI and Jamaat-e-Islami go for such strikes because they want the attention of the crowd. They deliberately create problems to fan communal hatred,' he says.

The proximity to Mahe poses another challenge, he goes on. The police then can't search immediately for the culprits because Mahe is a Union territory. If the killers flee there, they are able to escape the police radar. The availability of cheap liquor and drugs smuggled from Mahe to Kannur through the sea route or through the river has also contributed to the rise in crime in the district. 'People under substance abuse and alcoholics are routinely used as hired guns,' a Thalassery-based police officer tells me in an interview.

The police and forensic officers say that they can often identify the political affiliation of the culprits from the stab wounds of the victim. The CPI(M) squads usually come in large groups and launch a no-holds-barred attack on their targets. Which is why their victims bear numerous cuts. The RSS-affiliated ones, who are often well-trained, go for precision killing, slashing the arteries on the wrists or the popliteal artery just behind the knee joint. Lately, most killers have been hurling bombs to disorient the victim and then hack them around the ankles before going for the head and the throat. The PFI killers even use surgical knives and often slash the victim across the belly so that he bleeds profusely to death. The use of surgical knives, physicians and forensic experts tell me, requires sufficient training. Unlike swords and other traditional weapons, these cannot be used by the untrained to 'produce results'. Most parties practise their killing styles using dogs and other animals, according to senior police officers and forensic surgeons I interviewed in Kannur.

The last of Jacob's main theories for the political violence in Kannur was a lack of communication between police personnel—but thanks to the advent of cell phones and the Internet, this hurdle has been eased in the past decade or so.

Regarding the RSS's assertion that the CPI(M) has an axe to grind with all parties, while the RSS has a problem with only one party—the CPI(M)—Jacob avers that cases involving the RSS have been on the rise: with the Janata Dal; with the Muslim League; and with the PFI. Between 1971 and August 2017, he says, in the whole of Kerala, the CPI(M) lost 527 workers to the mindless violence, while all other parties put together lost 442 workers, of which the RSS–BJP–ABVP lost 185 people.

The RSS leader Nandakumar, meanwhile, tells me that his organization doesn't believe in talking of death through numbers. But Kannur's statistics defy pan-Kerala figures, and perhaps add to the RSS arsenal. In direct political clashes between the BJP–RSS and the CPI(M)–DYFI since 1984 in Kannur (data before that is not available with the district police), of the total ninety-three killed, fifty-three were from the Sangh and forty were Marxists.[18]

As the character Griffin says in *Men in Black III*, 'Where there is death, there will always be death.'

9

The Thorny Road Ahead

On the morning of 30 July 2016,[1] within two months of him taking over as chief minister, Pinarayi Vijayan, accompanied by leaders Kodiyeri Balakrishnan and V. Sivankutty, broke protocol and drove down to Mascot Hotel, a heritage building that once housed British officers during the First World War. There was no pilot jeep and no security paraphernalia accompanying them. It was a pre-planned meeting. Vijayan's mission was to meet Kummanam Rajasekharan, the Kerala president of the BJP; O. Rajagopal, the veteran BJP leader and lone legislator of his party in the state assembly; and Gopalankutty Master, an RSS heavyweight in the state. The sole agenda of the meeting was to find ways to make peace.

Such a meeting was considered unthinkable and was not disclosed to the media for a while, for there was a mutual understanding to keep these talks low profile; the intention was to gradually communicate the need to bring the rank and file on to the same page. It had to be confidential, and the attempt was to thrash out, step by step, ways to bury the hatchet between the extremely hostile cadres on both sides.

The man who moderated the meet was Sri M, the Kerala-born, Madanapalle-based spiritual leader who is close to the RSS chief Mohan Bhagwat as well as Vijayan and Balakrishnan.

After the leaders exchanged morning pleasantries and settled down to business, Sri M explained the purpose of the meeting—the violence that has scarred the state for decades, and taking place mostly in the chief minister's home district of Kannur, could not go on. Just that month in Kannur, after two consecutive murders of CPI(M) workers, a BMS leader was hacked to death in front of his family. It is also a fact that political murders rise in years when the CPI(M) and its allies are in power, and go down during the years of Congress rule—a number that is used by the Sangh to paint the Left as violent, and by the Marxists to indicate the increase in vicious provocation from the right wing.

For a state with the highest levels of literacy, a state with social indices comparable to Nordic countries, such violence was inexcusable, Sri M said, adding that one mustn't engage in a blame game about 'who started it' if the goal was to make peace. The ongoing cycle of bloody madness had no place in God's Own Country, the catchphrase sold the world over to attract tourists. In such a highly aware, networked, considerably urbanized society, even a single death should make its leaders hang their heads in shame, he went on. The past was past. One couldn't have yesterdays impinge on tomorrows; it was time for reconciliation and give and take. A consensus to save lives of men across the political spectrum was long overdue; the political will to weed out this menace could not wait any longer, the sage goaded.

But the meeting did not get off to a good start.

The RSS's Gopalankutty Master was in a belligerent mood; he had his set of grievances and tons of pessimism about the negotiations that were going on. Despite repeated assurances over the decades, peace had remained elusive. He felt—as I understood after I met with him—that whenever the Marxists had come to power, the RSS, at least since the late 1980s, had been singled out for barbaric strikes by the CPI(M). Apparently, he sat with his legs crossed in a manner that was not only meant to be disrespectful to a chief minister—who also held the charge of the home portfolio—but also combative.

To everyone's surprise, though, the otherwise irascible Vijayan smiled and agreed to hear him out. The tone of the meeting changed. Sri M intervened mildly to suggest that blaming one another would take the participants nowhere.

Soon, sensing the chief minister's apparent preparedness to engage, Gopalankutty Master mellowed.

The idea behind keeping the high-level, unofficial rendezvous between the top leaders on both sides under wraps had also to do with the fact that people on either side could play spoilsport. After all, there were leaders, sidekicks and gangsters with strong party affiliations who thrived, thanks to the violence.

The leaders dispersed after agreeing to convince their cadres about a ceasefire, as best as possible.

Both the RSS–BJP and the CPI(M) leaders would meet again, even in Kannur, but—despite the good beginning as is evident from the readiness to talk—the killings have shown no signs of subsiding yet. The trajectory of political assertion in Kannur and the nearby districts has shown no change of track. On the other hand, there are charges that there's an effort to import the 'Kannur model of politics' to the southern parts of the state as the RSS versus CPI(M) confrontations have begun to surface elsewhere, especially in Thiruvananthapuram where the BJP has been making some gains.

In such a situation, the optimism engendered by the government-initiated talks soon wore away.

The CPI(M) leaders believe that the RSS side hopes to reap benefits and make inroads into their turf by creating martyrs. The Marxists also hit out at the national campaigners of the RSS for seeking to generate optics as part of a nationwide campaign to taint opposition parties. They are of the view that the Sangh leaders in the state are simultaneously emboldened by their prospects nationally and crestfallen about their relatively slow gains in Kerala.

The RSS and the BJP lay the blame on the chief minister for his alleged failure to clamp down on the political murders in the state. While a section of their leaders based out of Delhi called for imposition of President's rule in the state—one of them appealed to the RSS men in Kerala to gouge out the eyes of the CPI(M) cadres—the RSS men in the state offered a more balanced comment. Gopalankutty Master put such frivolous remarks to rest by stating that officially, the RSS was against dismissing the state government.

To those outside Kerala, the Redtrocity campaign has ensured the projection of a distorted image of the ground reality where the selective emphasis on the RSS versus CPI(M) narrative has completely submerged the violence generated by the Congress, the PFI, the Muslim League and other parties. Using their considerable 'WhatsApp army', the right-wingers in other parts of India have continuously painted a picture of the CPI(M) as the 'butcher' of Kannur. The CPI(M),[2] on its part, has no campaign machinery at the national level, something which Pinarayi Vijayan concedes.[3] This is not to suggest that making the violence in Kannur an issue worthy of national debate has to be discouraged. The idea, as Nandakumar of the RSS himself tells me, is to let the truth out.

Though it is widely accepted that the registration of crimes in Kerala is high, the higher incidence of political crimes is a matter of grave concern. The state ranks third in crimes whose motives are attributed to 'political' reasons. In 2016, Kerala (with fifteen deaths) ranked third after Uttar Pradesh (twenty-nine) and Bihar (twenty-seven).[4] This is paradoxical for a state whose social indices are comparable to that of the developed nations. For instance, dowry-related death was zero in the state in 2016 (in Jharkhand it was thirty-seven). Similarly, there have been almost no killings over caste, honour, love affairs and class conflicts (133 people were killed over love affairs in Gujarat in 2016; in Rajasthan, sixteen people died that year in class conflicts). Nor does water or money really create enmity here—while forty-five people were killed in Gujarat in disputes over these issues in 2016, in Kerala the figure stood at one. As for rape-related deaths in 2016, Kerala reported two, Maharashtra nineteen and Madhya Pradesh eighteen.

Besides, when it comes to Kerala, it isn't as easy as it sounds for the ruling CPI(M) to 'influence' the murder cases with the help of the police. Most of the senior police officers, says former DGP Alexander Jacob, are apparently Congress or BJP supporters. It is only in the lower rungs of the police force that the CPI(M) holds sway. Vijayan has even come under attack in his party's district-level conferences for failing to lasso senior officers of the state police who, they allege, are out to tarnish the chief minister's image.

And so, if one glances even cursorily at claims by non-Kerala players in painting the state as a haven for murderers— and especially the contention that the communists are out to get the RSS–BJP workers—it is easy to see these are more or less politically motivated, and are not entirely based on truth.

Last year in Kannur, a group of assailants pounced on a local leader of the BJP, Sushil Kumar, attacking him with a sharp blade akin to a surgical knife. Kumar was seriously injured, but he survived. He lost no time in blaming the CPI(M) for this attempt on his life—and even claimed that he saw and knew some of his attackers. The initial probe led to a list of pro-Marxist hired guns he had 'identified'. After a few rounds of interrogation, the police decided that Kumar could be wrong about the men who had stabbed him.

Surgical knives obtained from medical stores had been used against a Muslim League worker in the district some time earlier, prompting the cops to examine the link between the two acts of crime. Weeks of investigation led to the arrests of workers of the Campus Front, a feeder outfit of the PFI. The Kannur town DSP, P. Sadanandan, who was part of the investigating team, tells me that this attack on Kumar followed a spate of clashes between the Campus Front activists and the ABVP students who often brought in RSS toughies to the College of Commerce, a 'parallel college' (a private tuition centre of sorts) in town, to intimidate their rivals. The Campus Front members who were caught also complained that they were routinely harassed outside the campus by BJP–RSS workers.[5] Yet, despite such constant bickering between the ABVP and the Campus Front in that part of the town, the Sangh student leader decided to name CPI(M) men as his attackers; he also claimed that he could identify some of them, but then retracted his statement when the police called his bluff.

DSP Sadanandan had been involved in the investigation of the T.P. Chandrasekharan murder case of 2012 which led to linking one of the accused, T.K. Rajeesh, who owed allegiance to the CPI(M), to earlier killings, including that of K.T. Jayakrishnan Master of the RSS.

There is no doubt that the CPI(M) has done its share in turning Kannur into a political battlefield, and the killings of T.P. Chandrasekharan—leader of a breakaway group, the RMP—and Ariyil Shukoor are a testimony to that. Shukoor was killed a few hours after he and a few other Muslim League workers had allegedly attacked a vehicle in which CPI(M) district secretary P. Jayarajan and other party workers were travelling, on 20 February 2012, near Taliparamba. Shukoor was killed in Kannapuram, while his associate suffered stab injuries in the same assault.[6] The case is being probed by the CBI.

But not all murders in the area have had to do with the CPI(M), as some national campaigns suggest. Earlier in 2012, another ABVP leader, Sachin Gopalan,[7] (see Chapter 1) was killed by the Campus Front activists. Prior to that, in 2005, as explained earlier, thirty-year-old Ashwini Kumar of the RSS, who was also the Hindu Aikya Vedi district secretary, was bumped off by suspected workers of the National Development Front (NDF), avatar of the PFI. In retaliation, many Muslim homes in Iritty where Kumar was killed were torched and looted. Deep fissures within the district RSS over the issue meant that there were rumours about a 'financial settlement' between the top brass of the RSS district leadership and the NDF. And yet, several RSS leaders blamed the CPI(M) for the attack.

On 19 January 2018, a three-member gang of suspected PFI men slew Shyam Prasad, an Industrial Training Institute (ITI) student, on his way back to his home in Koothuparamba on a bike at a place called Kommeri at around 5.30 p.m. He died on his way to the hospital. Several RSS men in and out of Kerala charged the CPI(M) with the attack though initial reports had made it amply clear who the attackers were. The PFI versus RSS clashes are now as common as the RSS versus IUML clashes earlier. Raghav Pandey, a research fellow with the Department of Humanities and Social Sciences (IIT Bombay), even used the occasion to launch into a tirade against communist atrocities and Stalinism.[8]

The frequent murders in Kannur, followed by immediate political blame games, are ripe case-study material for criminal-law students wanting to know how perceptions are built around a crime. In a case involving the murder of PFI activist Mohammad Fazal that is being probed by the CBI, and in the process has courted controversy over its apparent lack of direction, the CPI(M) has alleged a witch-hunt by the investigation agency.

Inconsistencies in the probe by several independent agencies give credence to the CPI(M)'s version that both the RSS and the PFI are out to implicate them in murder cases because the communists are equally hostile to them both. Court records and CBI's own charge sheet in the case point to inconsistencies in the versions of key witnesses to the crime that took place between 3 and 4 a.m. on 22 October 2006. Witnesses had later said that they were asked to lie to the police by a National Democratic Front (NDF) lawyer[9] and say that it was not the RSS but CPI(M) workers who were behind Fazal's murder. Ajnas and Shahnad, two NDF workers who claimed to have witnessed the killing, later reversed their statement. In fact, one of them was in Coimbatore at the time of the murder.

More importantly, the police are in possession of a video disclosure by RSS worker Subeesh, an accused in the murder of CPI(M)'s K. Mohanan at Valankichal. In an indiscreet moment, Subeesh spoke to an RSS leader about

Fazal's murder on the phone; the audio clip of the chat was leaked, probably by some rivals within the Sangh. He is heard telling the RSS leader, an audio that I was able to listen to, that in a bid to escape, Fazal had tried to break through the grills of a home. Subeesh goes on to describe all the details of the escape attempt to the RSS leader. After questioning by the police, Subeesh later publicly confessed that a group of RSS workers, including him, were involved in the murder of Fazal. Ever since, the CBI inquiry into the case has hit a roadblock.[10]

The web of complex lies spun to implicate CPI(M) leaders has attracted much ridicule in local conversations, and given rise to several social-media memes and jokes on the subject, one of which depicts two RSS and NDF men fighting and crying while pointing accusing fingers at a CPI(M) passer-by. On a serious note, however, the botched CBI case strengthens the CPI(M) argument that their rivals lose no opportunity in framing and maligning them as part of a political agenda to weaken the party. However, given its own history of violence, the CPI(M) has been, as it seems, unable to gain political mileage from it.

Political concerns must not be allowed to distract from the humanitarian tragedy unfolding in one of India's most progressive states.[11] There are many solutions to end the serial violence in the district but all need political and community will at both state and national levels. Alexander Jacob is of the view that a Kannur Regiment has to be created to tap the aggression of youths in the region for nation-building purposes, the way the Indian army accelerated recruitment into the Naga Regiment to tackle the insurgency in Nagaland. This has been pitched as one of the most effective strategies in bringing down the complex waves of militancy plaguing the north-eastern state where there's a demand for regional autonomy.

To me, however, a more viable solution for Kannur lies in its local history, in understanding where the residents came from and how they lived, especially when the practice of kalaripayattu was instilled as a discipline among young people. According to S.R.D. Prasad, a kalaripayattu guru and author of an encyclopedia on the martial-art form, that was also part of the judicial system of the day. He advocates promoting the discipline as a sport, which, he says, could work as an antidote in combating political crime. Unlike earlier, when kalaripayattu was a way of life in these parts, these days there are very few practitioners. Young people have no avenues to channel their excess energy, he maintains. Northern Kerala, especially Kannur, is home to abrasive sport forms such as *adiyutsavam*, an annual event held at the

Mavilayi Kavu, a place of worship, in which people engage in mock fights that can inflict terrible injury. Incidentally, Mavilayi is the birthplace of the great Marxist leader A.K. Gopalan. But with its history, code of defence and emphasis on personal discipline, kalaripayattu is better suited to the temperament of the local population. Making it a lucrative commercial sport such as by staging a Kalaripayattu Premier League would be an even better solution. It would galvanize young men, generate employment and—one hopes—convert testosterone-driven aggression into a multi-crore industry.

Proactively offering space in leadership to women and peaceniks to counter the toxic masculinity in Kannur's politics is another prospective strategy for the state's political and thought leaders to consider. As of now, female voices and votaries of peace among male leaders often get sidelined in favour of ferocious, adrenaline-stirred functionaries—a trend that cuts across the political spectrum. An absence of such measures will only dent the prospects of safeguarding democracy and lead to a loss of credibility of organizations.

Several police bigwigs, including Alexander Jacob and Sadanandan, accept that the state police needs serious introspection and resurrection. Facing an acute shortage in personnel, the police either go by the 'list of perpetrators' supplied by the victims' side or that of the accused. Such cosmetic investigations, wherein the police and parties stay hand in glove for the sake of convenience, mean that the real culprits often get away and are, in fact, encouraged to keep doing what they do best: murder.

While it is heartening that, of late, the culprits are being nabbed with great alacrity, the top priority ought to be on enhancing the strength of the police force in the district, and speeding up the investigation process. A far more heightened but facts-oriented campaign to highlight the plight of the families of the dead is also in order to name and shame the parties that encourage violence—which, as of now, is entirely political and not communal. Besides, utmost attention has to be paid to the communal forces that take advantage of the political clashes—which, unfortunately, is now taking place frequently.

Outside most crematoriums in Kerala, relatives of the deceased offer handfuls of rice (*bali-chor*) to resident crows that are called *bali kakakal*. A traditional belief is that their ancestors accept food and offerings through these birds, and their presence is auspicious.

Standing at Payyambalam beach graveyard, I can see smoke billowing from the firewood stacked up at the local crematorium less than 50 metres away. As the grey wisps rise, I am reminded of Joseph Conrad's imageries of the Congo and the soulless self-interests of its predatory men in *Heart of Darkness.*

Hope seems to go up in flames into the melancholy dusk. The crows are nowhere to be seen.

Acknowledgements

I would like to thank Penguin and my commissioning editor, Premanka Goswami, for inviting me to write this book. My home town, Kannur, has been a hot topic in the national media of late, and it is a matter of destiny that I was born into a family deeply rooted in local politics. While I did fall back on memory, folklore and traditional knowledge in the writing of this book, I also travelled across Kerala to conduct several face-to-face interviews cutting across party lines for the purpose of giving a balanced viewpoint.

I would like to thank the following people who gave me their valuable time and on-record interviews. Many of them are also personal acquaintances and all have my heartfelt gratitude for their inputs over the years.

Acknowledgements

- Pinarayi Vijayan, chief minister of Kerala
- J. Nandakumar, national convener of prajna pravah, and all-India executive committee member of the RSS. He is also the architect of the Redtrocity campaign.
- Pattiam Rajan, former CPI(M) leader and Rajya Sabha member
- P. Narayanan, RSS leader and ideologue
- R. Hari, RSS leader and ideologue
- P. Jayarajan, CPI(M) district committee secretary, Kannur
- P.P. Suresh Babu, RSS leader
- Sri M, spiritual guru
- K.N. Govindacharya, RSS stalwart
- M.V. Govindan Master, CPI(M) state secretariat member
- Churayi Chandran, former CPI(M) leader and educationist
- Valsan Thillenkeri, RSS leader
- Alexander Jacob, former director general of police (prisons), Kerala
- T. Purushothaman, CPI leader and entrepreneur
- A. Ashokan, former BJP leader who is now with the CPI(M)
- O.K. Vasu, former BJP leader who is now with the CPI(M)
- P. Sadanandan, officer with the Kerala Police

- K. Sanil Kumar, former leader of CPI(M)'s youth wing in Kannur
- A.N. Shamseer, CPI(M) leader and MLA from Thalassery
- Babu, a Kannur-based kalaripayattu practitioner and trainer
- S.R.D. Prasad, kalaripayattu guru
- Professor T. Sasidharan, author and expert on Kannur's political violence; he is also the head of department of political science at Sree Narayana College, Kannur. He is the author of *Idathupakshavum Kannur Rashtreeyavum*, whose updated version was later translated into English as *Radical Politics of Kannur.*
- Chandrasekharan, a Thalassery-based veteran leader of the RSS
- I.V. Shivaraman, former area secretary, Madayi CPI(M), Kannur
- Anil Edathil, a Thalassery resident and businessman
- O.V. Abdullah, a Thalassery-born Middle East-based business tycoon
- E.M. Abdul Rahiman, PFI leader
- Manoj Mathan, former SFI leader, and entrepreneur
- Dr N.K. Purushothaman, social activist
- Vanidas Elayavoor, scholar and teacher
- N. Ramakrishnan, the late Congress leader and former Kerala minister (1997)

- M.V. Raghavan, the late CPI(M) leader who broke away and floated his new party, CMP; he was also a minister in the Kerala government (1998)

I also met the relatives of people who had fallen victim to the vendetta killings in Kannur; besides numerous others from various political parties and social organizations in Kerala who did not wish to be named.

I would like to thank my editor at *Open* magazine, R. Prasannarajan, for his support and for endowing the book's title, and my friends, John Brittas, Praveen S. Thampi, Siddharth Singh, Dinesh Narayanan, Anu Narayanan, Priya K. Nair, Sunil Kumar, Anil G. Nair and Vazhayil Babu.

As an insider to Kannur politics and society, I had both the advantage of knowing untold secrets and the disadvantage of carrying the burden of unconscious bias. And so I am deeply indebted to my mother, N.K. Mridula, for her insights and still-sharp memory, and to my wife, Aekta Kapoor, for her tough questions that ensured I kept my perspective as neutral as possible.

Notes

1. Waves of Violence

1. In 2005, V.S. Achuthanandan, the then opposition leader in the Kerala assembly, criticized the ruling dispensation. Replying to questions, he said the CPI(M) continued to believe that Karunakaran had an important role in the murder of Azhikodan Raghavan. 'CPI(M) Claims Credit for Fall of Naxalism in State', *The Hindu*, 23 February 2005, http://www.thehindu.com/2005/09/23/stories/2005092309950500.htm.

2. The CPI split in 1964 over the issue of a softer approach towards the ruling Congress of the time; some leaders argued that the party should align with the national bourgeoisie to take on extremism and fundamentalism of all kinds. Thirty-three members of the CPI's national council walked out, ruling out any truck with the Congress, and formed a new entity, later christened as Communist

Party of India (Marxist), or CPI(M). The Congress was in alliance for ten years with the CPI between 1970 and 1980 before the latter returned to the Left camp.

3. While the district of Kannur is known for its pristine natural beauty, sadly the region is replete with political murders, which attract massive media coverage. During my interview with Alexander Jacob, I was able to understand the severity and gravity of the violence in a unique way.

4. *Moyarath Sankaran: Autobiography of a Freedom Fighter and a Martyr*, translated by Radhika P. Menon (Thiruvananthapuram: Chintha Publishers, 2016).

5. Ibid.

6. For further reading, refer to Saqib Khan's article in *EPW Engage*: 'A "Reading" without History: Questioning a Flawed Reading of Left Politics in Tripura', http://www.epw.in/engage/article/reading-without-history-questioning-flawed-reading-left-politics-tripura.

7. Also refer to Ranadive's *Caste, Class, and Property Relation* (Calcutta: National Book Agency, 1982). In addition, *B.T. Ranadive on Trade Union Movement* (vols 1–3), published by the Centre of Indian Trade Unions (CITU) in 1990, would offer insights.

8. K. Satchidanandan in his article, 'Words Were His Soldiers', remembers the life, times and works of Azhikode. *The Hindu*, 2 February 2012, http://www.thehindu.com/opinion/op-ed/words-were-his-soldiers/article2851360.ece.

9. Alison Saldanha, Gangadhar Patil, 'In Kannur, RSS–BJP and CPI(M) Have Lost Equal Numbers to Political Violence', Scroll, 7 March 2017, https://scroll.in/article/831083/in-kannur-rss-bjp-and-cpi-m-have-lost-equal-numbers-to-political-violence.

10. Though the RSS set up its unit in Kerala as early as 1942, its political arm, the BJP, or its earlier avatar, the BJS, has so far won only one seat in the state assembly, and that too as late as in the last elections of 2016. And in Kannur district, the percentage of votes the BJP won in the last assembly election was much less than its state average.

11. This is based on data accessed from the district crime records bureau, Kannur.

12. According to news reports and political analyses in regional weeklies of that time, the RSS offered protection to the beedi companies, Guru Kripa and Mahalaxmi, which were started by the Mangalore-based M. Govinda Rao and partners, after they shut down Ganesh Beedi's operations in Kannur. Guru Kripa ran its units in and around the Kanhangad area of the then Kannur district, and Mahalaxmi in Thalassery.

13. John Mary, 'Violence as Political Tool Keeps Cadre Intact', *Deccan Chronicle*, 13 August 2017, https://www. deccanchronicle.com/360-degree/130817/violence-as-political-tool-keeps-cadre-intact.html.

14. 'ABVP Activist's Murder: 10 Identified', *The Hindu*, 15 September 2012, http://www.thehindu.com/todays-paper/ tp-national/tp-kerala/abvp-activists-murder-10-identified/ article3899718.ece.

2. First Blood

1. For an interesting read on the political violence in Kannur, see Monu Rajan's 'Entering the Fort Red', *The Hindu BusinessLine*, 6 November 2017, https://www.thehindubusinessline.com/ specials/india-file/entering-the-fort-red/article9945733.ece. Also my own story on political violence, 'Pinarayi Vijayan:

The McMarxist from Malabar', *Open*, 3 June 2016, http://
www.openthemagazine.com/article/india/pinarayi-vijayan-
the-mcmarxist-from-malabar.

2. Meen Aviyal, 'How the Right-biased Media Is Trying to Paint
   Kerala as a Communal Warzone', DailyO, 3 February 2017,
   https://www.dailyo.in/politics/bjp-rss-right-wing-media-is-
   trying-to-paint-kerala-as-communal-warzone/story/1/15469.
   html. You may also refer to Sam Jawed's 'Malicious Attempts
   to Portray K.R. Narayanan, India's First Dalit President, as a
   Christian', Alt News, 28 July 2017, https://www.altnews.in/
   malicious-attempts-portray-k-r-narayanan-indias-first-dalit-
   president-christian/.

3. 'Pinarayi Vijayan, the Prime Accused in Kerala's First Political
   Murder?', PGurus, 16 October 2017, https://www.pgurus.
   com/pinarayi-vijayan-the-prime-accused-in-keralas-first-
   political-murder/.

4. Ibid.

5. Kaviyoor Balan, *Kathi Theeratha Innalekal* (Thalassery:
   Thalassery Arts Society, 2017).

6. Karl Marx, Friedrich Engels, *The Communist Manifesto* (1848).

7. I met P. Sasi for this interview in 1993. He had made a name
   as a student leader, who would later fall victim to carnal
   indiscretions, resulting in his expulsion from the party. He is
   now a highly successful lawyer.

8. Based on interviews with the likes of senior CPI(M) leader
   M.V. Govindan on 1 January 2018.

9. Nidheesh M.K., 'The Curious Similarities between Pinarayi
   Vijayan and Narendra Modi', *LiveMint*, 3 June 2016, http://
   www.livemint.com/Politics/7VaeyWsVcn04MA915FE2qI/
   The-curious-similarities-between-Pinarayi-Vijayan-and-
   Narend.html.

10. Dinesh Narayanan, 'BJP Ups the Ante in CPI(M)'s Backyard as It Eyes Electoral Opportunity in Kerala', *Economic Times*, 8 October 2017, https://economictimes.indiatimes.com/news/politics-and -nation/march-of-saffron-in-the-land-of-red/ articleshow/60986679.cms.

11. Based on my interviews with Pinarayi Vijayan in 2016 and 2017.

12. Kurup, who had been minister twice in the CPI(M)-led governments in Kerala (in 1967 and 1996), had in 1973 joined the Congress; a few years later, he quit the Congress and joined the Janata Party. See also Mohamed Nazeer's 'A Merger at Panur, Four Decades Ago', *The Hindu*, 29 January 2014, http://www. thehindu.com/news/national/kerala/a-merger-at-panur-four-decades-ago/article5627179.ece.

13. T.N. Sasidharan, the head of the political science department (Sree Narayana College, Kannur), has exhaustively researched the history of political violence in Kannur. Historically, the murder of Ramakrishnan is treated as the starting point of political murders in the district, but as Sasidharan argues, the genesis of political violence began with the emergence of the PSP in the 1950s under P.R. Kurup. Refer to the following article: 'Politics of Violence: Kannur Witnessed 186 Murders', *Economic Times*, 8 March 2017, https://economictimes.indiatimes.com/news/politics-and-nation/politics-of-violence-kannur-witnessed-186-murders/articleshow/57532865.cms.

14. Government of Kerala archives.

15. Based on my interviews with Pinarayi Vijayan in 2016 and 2017.

16. T.M. Thomas Isaac, Richard W. Franke and Pyaralal Raghavan, *Democracy at Work in an Indian Industrial Cooperative: Story of Kerala Dinesh Beedi* (New York: Cornell University Press, 1998).

17. Uday Mahurkar, 'Bound by Traditional Values, Rs 3,000-cr Beedi Industry Now Sees Winds of Change Blowing', *India Today*, 15 November 1989, https://www.indiatoday.in/magazine/economy/story/19891115-bound-by-traditional-values-rs-3000-cr-beedi-industry-now-sees-winds-of-change-blowing-816745-1989-11-15.

18. Thomas Isaac, Richard W. Franke and Pyaralal Raghavan, *Democracy at Work in an Indian Industrial Cooperative.*

19. For further discussion on this, refer to Sujata Anandan's *Samrat: How the Shiv Sena Changed Mumbai Forever* (Noida: HarperCollins Publishers India, 2014).

20. Published in the *Economic and Political Weekly* on 30 April 2005.

3. Vignettes of Grief and Rage

1. 'Revenge Killing Again? Kerala RSS Man Accused in Political Murder, Hacked to Death', News Minute, 12 May 2017, https://www.thenewsminute.com/article/revenge-killing-again-rss-worker-accused-political-murder-hacked-death-broad-daylight-61918.

2. You may like to go through my article 'The Comrade Who Dared (1933 to 2014)', *Open*, 11 November 2014, http://www.openthemagazine.com/article/india/the-comrade-who-dared-mv-raghavan-1933-to-2014. Besides, you may look at Shaju Philip's 'M V Raghavan, Communist Leader Who Took On CPM in Kerala, Passes Away', *Indian Express*, 10 November 2014, http://indianexpress.com/article/india/politics/m-v-raghavan-communist-leader-who-took-on-cpm-in-kerala-dead/.

3. https://twitter.com/AmitShah/status/786162941645164549.

4. 'Revenge Killing Again? Kerala RSS Man Accused in Political Murder, Hacked to Death', News Minute, 12 May 2017, https://www.thenewsminute.com/article/revenge-killing-again-rss-worker-accused-political-murder-hacked-death-broad-daylight-61918.
5. 'Arrested Shuhaib's Murder Suspect Is CPM "Cyber Warrior"', Manoramaonline, 19 February 2018, http://english.manoramaonline.com/news/kerala/2018/02/19/arrested-shuhaib-murder-suspect-cpm-cyber-warrior.html.
6. P. Sudhakaran, 'BJP Worker Hacked to Death in Kerala's Kannur', *Times of India*, 19 January 2017, https://timesofindia.indiatimes.com/city/kozhikode/bjp-worker-hacked-to-death-in-kannur/articleshow/56657547.cms.
7. Interviews with P. Jayarajan (September 2017); police and medical reports; and his book, *Sangharshangalude Rashtreeyam: Fascisathinte Asooravazhikal* (The Politics of Conflict: Demonic Reign of Fascism), (Thiruvananthapuram: Chintha Publishers, 2008).
8. You may look at Anoop Parameshwaran's and Achyuth Punnekat's article 'Kerala CPM Sidelines Kannur Strongman for "Promoting Himself over Party"', News18, 13 November 2017, http://www.news18.com/news/politics/kerala-cpm-sidelines-kannur-strongman-for-promoting-himself-over-party-1575683.html. Also see 'Threat Made to Chop Off CPI(M) Leader's Hand at BJP Kerala Rally', News Minute, 10 October 2017, https://www.thequint.com/news/politics/threat-made-to-chop-off-cpim-leaders-hand-at-bjp-kerala-rally.
9. https://www.youtube.com/watch?v=56K6bGLIB4A.
10. *Kannurinte Kanneer* (Kannur's Tears), speech series by Valsan Thillenkeri on the history of CPI(M) violence in Kannur, https://www.youtube.com/watch?v=vuG92EY5fTA.

11. https://www.youtube.com/watch?v=a5CnF_gCde4.

12. My article, 'The Blood Sport of Malabar', *Open*, 12 September 2014, http://www.openthemagazine.com/article/india/the-bloodsport-of-malabar.

13. C. Gouridasan Nair, 'Who's Behind the Kerala Killings?', *The Hindu*, 10 March 2017, http://www.thehindu.com/opinion/op-ed/whos-behind-the-kerala-killings/article17436566.ece.

14. Shahina K.K., 'A Familiar Murderer in the PTA', *Open*, 12 November 2012, http://www.openthemagazine.com/shorts/smallworld/a-familiar-murderer-in-the-pta.

15. https://www.youtube.com/watch?v=sDc1CIvofNQ.

16. S-shaped knives were typically used by Samurais and killers for churning inside a person's body to damage multiple internal organs and to ensure that the enemy died.

17. Chintha Mary Anil, 'CPI(M) Cadres Hacked His Legs Off in '94, Now Sadanandan Master Is Back as a BJP Candidate', News Minute, 24 March 2016, https://www.thenewsminute.com/article/cpim-cadres-hacked-his-legs-94-now-sadanandan-master-back-bjp-candidate-40744.

18. Mohamed Nazeer, 'Songs of Blood and Sword in Kannur', *The Hindu*, 11 May 2016, http://www.thehindu.com/elections/kerala2016/songs-of-blood-and-sword-in-kannur/article8581836.ece.

19. 'The Blood Sport of Malabar', *Open*, 12 September 2014, http://www.openthemagazine.com/article/india/the-blood-sport-of-malabar.

20. In the newly reconstituted RSS organizational hierarchy in Kerala, 'vibhag' represents a revenue district. The RSS now has fourteen vibhags in the state, one in each district, as opposed to six or so earlier. The RSS's zillas are therefore almost the size of its earlier talukas. There is a new panel called *khand*, below the

zillas. A khand is made up of several mandals which comprise many shakhas, the smallest units. This reconfiguration is aimed at streamlining the activities of the Sangh and its affiliates in the states.

4. The Spell of the Northern Ballads

1. T. Sasidharan, *Idathupakshavum Kannur Rashtreeyavum* (Radical Politics of Kannur), (Kozhikode: Mathrubhumi Books, 2012).

5. The Flag-Bearers

1. The United Provinces in pre-independence India referred approximately to the areas that now comprise Uttar Pradesh and Uttarakhand.
2. Thomas Johnson Nossiter, *Communism in Kerala: A Study in Political Adaptation* (Berkeley: University of California Press, 1982).
3. For more, visit www.cpimkerala.org.
4. R. Krishnakumar, 'A Man and a Movement', *Frontline*, 14–27 August 2004, http://www.frontline.in/static/html/fl2117/stories/20040827003109700.htm.
5. Ibid.
6. Published by C Hurst & Co Publishers Ltd in 1982.
7. For EMS's speeches, visit www.cpimkerala.org.
8. R. Krishnakumar, 'A Man and a Movement', *Frontline*.
9. Thomas Johnson Nossiter's *Communism in Kerala* discusses how Congress and the Kerala Congress organized Paura Samithi (Citizens' Group) and the communists, Gopala Sena.

10. The Telangana struggle was originally launched by peasants against the wily Razakhars and the Nizam of Hyderabad. The communist party liberated 3000 villages and redistributed 1 million acres of land to the people; but after the Indian forces entered these areas in 1948, they clamped down on the communists, resulting in the loss of more than 4000 lives and the capture of more than 50,000 people.

11. Shaju Philip, 'MV Raghavan, Communist Leader Who Took on CPM in Kerala, Passes Away', *Indian Express*, 10 November 2014, http://indianexpress.com/article/india/politics/m-v-raghavan-communist-leader-who-took-on-cpm-in-kerala-dead/.

12. Mohamed Nazeer, 'Discord in MVR Family to the Fore', *The Hindu*, 6 May 2016, http://www.thehindu.com/news/national/kerala/discord-in-mvr-family-to-the-fore/article8563514.ece.

6. Congress versus the Communists

1. MVR and his associates were suspended in 1986 and eventually sacked for secretly circulating an alternative political document that prescribed an alliance with the Muslim League as an antidote to ending time in the opposition ranks and to cruise to power in the state. Their argument, after remaining in the Opposition for a long time, was that the party cannot sustain itself and work for the cause of the people without forming a government.

2. T. Sasidharan, the head of the political science department of Sree Narayana College, Kannur, is an authority on the history of the political violence in Kannur. His book, *Idathupakshavum Kannur Rashtreeyavum*, published by the

Kozhikode-based Mathrubhumi Books in 2012, looks at the socio-economic factors responsible for the violence. In fact, he throws light on the emergence of the PSP in the 1950s and the role of P.R. Kurup.

3. Ibid.

4. Churayi Chandran, former CPI(M) leader and educationist (phone interviews in 2017 and 2018).

5. The case proved to be a fictitious one. The affairs of the ISRO unit in Kerala didn't come under the state government, so there was no point in blaming Chief Minister Karunakaran. But the media onslaught and the Congress high command's growing dislike of Karunakaran, once a staunch ally of Indira Gandhi, resulted in his exit from the ministry.

6. When the Left was in power 1987–91, only a single CMP member made it to the assembly and that was MVR himself, from Azhikode.

7. 'K. Sudhakaran Accused of Plotting to Kill E.P. Jayarajan', *The Hindu*, 1 July 2012, http://www.thehindu.com/todays-paper/k-sudhakaran-accused-of-plotting-to-kill-ep-jayarajan/article3590681.ece.

7. The Religion Card

1. At the shakhas, volunteers are given physical and, sometimes, arms training, and intellectual discourses are conducted. Women are not allowed, although a few districts do have separate shakhas for women.

2. Jyoti Basu, '60 Years of Our Independence and the Left: Some Thoughts', *People's Democracy*, 19 August 2007, https://archives.peoplesdemocracy.in/2007/0819/08192007_jyoti%20basu.htm.

3. During my interview with Ranga Hari in 2017.
4. Sanju Sadanandan and Nirupaka Bharati, eds, *Aahuti: The Untold Stories of Sacrifice in Kerala* (Bengaluru: Centre for Kerala Socio-economic and Political Studies, September 2016), http://www.bjp.org/images/pdf/Aahuti-English.pdf.
5. *Sanghacharithravali* (History of the Sangh), an RSS publication for internal circulation.
6. Rao would later head Vanvasi Kalyan, the feeder organization of the RSS that works among the tribals. He passed away in 2012.
7. My interviews with the veteran RSS leader Chandrasekharan.
8. My interviews with J. Nandakumar in 2016 and 2017.
9. Cited in *Kannurinte Kanneer*.
10. Yechury had written an exhaustive article on the book in 1993 after the RSS denied it was a book by Golwalkar. 'What Is Hindu Rashtra?', *Frontline*, 21 July 2017, http://www.frontline.in/cover-story/what-is-hindu-rashtra/article9748316.ece.
11. 'IUML Facilitated "Nexus" with BJP in 1991, says Murali', *The Hindu*, 24 September 2005, http://www.thehindu.com/2005/09/24/stories/2005092406530400.htm.
12. During the Emergency, both the RSS and CPI(M) leaders would find themselves in the same jail.
13. The Left's tally from Kannur was way above the average compared to a statewide rout of the CPI(M) and its allies; of the seventeen seats that the CPI(M) won in the state election, five were from Kannur and one from Kasaragod, which together fell under the undivided district committee of the CPI(M). Much credit goes to the Kannur unit of the CPI(M), which was far more active than the rest of the district panels, in disseminating information about the ills of the Emergency.

14. My article in *Open* magazine, 'Marching for Jihad', 20 October 2017, http://www.openthemagazine.com/article/cover-story/marching-for-jihad.
15. According to the RSS, there are 56,859 shakhas across the country.
16. My article in *Open* magazine, 'BJP's Next Target: Kerala', 13 March 2017, http://www.openthemagazine.com/article/politics/bjp-s-next-target-kerala.
17. *Aahuti*, http://www.bjp.org/images/pdf/Aahuti-English.pdf.

8. The Anatomy of a Conflict

1. This story comes up in a book on Kerala history prepared by Kerala Gazetteers, a government-run agency, edited by Adoor K.K. Ramachandran Nair in 1986; it has a foreword by the then chief minister K. Karunakaran.
2. Alexander Jacob was the assistant superintendent of police in Kannur in the mid-1980s, superintendent of police from 1988–89 and deputy inspector general of police (northern range) in the mid-1990s. An award-winning officer, he was also deputy inspector general (armed police battalion) before he became a DGP.
3. Kerala state records.
4. 'The Izhavas of Kerala and Their Historic Struggle for Acceptance in the Hindu Society', *Journal of Asian and African Studies*, vol. 11, 1976.
5. This has been noted by many academics, including Janaki Abraham of the Department of Sociology, Delhi School of Economics, whose work covered the well-to-do Thiyya families in Thalassery.

6. Interviews with Chief Minister Pinarayi Vijayan in 2016 and 2017.

7. Cited in *Kannurinte Kanneer*.

8. One may like to go through M.B. Rajesh's write-up, 'Red Terror or Saffron Shock in Kerala?', *Indian Express*, 8 August 2017, http://indianexpress.com/article/opinion/red-terror-or-saffron-shock-in-kerala-bjp-sangh-parivar-rss-cpi-m-arun-jaitley-4786803/; as well as my story, 'The Blood Sport of Malabar', *Open*, 12 September 2014.

9. The reality is much more complex, thanks to the British efforts to target Muslims and divide people along communal lines. Their strategy worked and several Hindus became victims of Muslim onslaught, resulting in widespread exodus and gruesome atrocities. Over the decades, there has been a concerted effort by a section of politicians and historians to portray the rebellion exclusively as an anti-Hindu riot.

10. P. Sudhakaran, 'How "India's James Bond" Ajit Doval Ended a 1971 Hindu–Muslim Riot in Just One Week', Indiatimes, 3 October 2016, https://www.indiatimes.com/news/india/how-india-s-james-bond-ajit-dobal-ended-a-1971-hindi-muslim-riot-in-just-one-week-262817.html.

11. I gathered this from various newspaper reports of the time and the police documents I was able to access.

12. Alexander Jacob, former director general of police (prisons), Kerala, said this during my interview with him in 2018.

13. Vasu and Ashokan disclosed this to me in separate interviews.

14. In north Kerala, like elsewhere, English words have acquired different meanings compared to the original. For instance, a vulgarized variant of 'mistake', pronounced 'mistikk', is used to refer to a cad or to things that go wrong.

15. *Times of India*, 18 January 2014, https://timesofindia. indiatimes.com/Police-have-recovered-36-bombs-from-Puthankandam-near-Venduttai-under-Kathirur-police-limits-in-Kannur-on-Saturday-afternoon-According-to-Kathiroor-police-35-were-powerful-steel-bombs-and-one-was-an-ice-cream-bomb-that-were-found-abandoned-in-a-vacant-plot-when-a-raid-was-conducted-based-on-a-tip-off-around-4-30-p-m-Some-gunpowder-was-also-recovered-from-a-nearby-plot-/articleshow/29015577.cms.

16. K. Janardhanan was an accused in a 1986 murder case and then spent time in jail. He later invited party disciplinary action when M.V. Govindan Master was the district secretary of the CPI(M); the primary charge was that of promoting a culture of violence among the young cadres. But he continues to be closely associated with some key party leaders.

17. The CPI(M) gangsters who were arrested have curious nicknames such as 'Kodi' (flag) Suni and 'Trouser' Manoj. The RSS goons also have similar monikers, such as 'Kaka' (crow) Shaji and 'Kabartheeni' (gravedigger) Ashokan. I mustered these from newspaper reports and conversations with police officers.

18. A reply to the author from the central information commission on 30 January 2018.

9. The Thorny Road Ahead

1. My interviews with Sri M and Pinarayi Vijayan in 2016 and 2017 respectively.

2. Debobrat Ghose, 'Kerala Political Violence: Is CPM Insecure about Modi Juggernaut Unseating It from Its Last Bastion?', Firstpost, 7 August 2017, http://www.firstpost.com/politics/kerala-political-violence-is-cpm-insecure-about-narendra-

modi-juggernaut-unseating-it-from-its-last-bastion-3901623. html. Also see 'Fazal Murder—BJP, PFI Dismiss Confession', *Times of India*, 23 November 2016, https://timesofindia. indiatimes.com/city/kozhikode/FAZAL-MURDER-BJP-PFI- dismiss-confession/articleshow/55573125.cms.

3. Pinarayi Vijayan gave me an interview at Cliff House, his official residence, in Thiruvananthapuram.

4. The source is the national crime records bureau's 'Crime in India 2016' (p. 93).

5. My article, 'Marching for Jihad', *Open*, 20 October 2017.

6. 'Timeline: HC Nod for CBI Probe in Shukoor Murder Yet Another Blow for CPI(M)', News Minute, 9 February 2016, https://www.thenewsminute.com/article/timeline-hc-nod- cbi-probe-shukoor-murder-yet-another-blow-cpim-38733.

7. 'One More PFI Activist Arrested in ABVP Activist Murder Case', *The Hindu*, 26 September 2012, http://www.thehindu. com/news/national/kerala/one-more-pfi-activist-arrested-in- abvp-activist-murder-case/article3938930.ece.

8. Raghav Pandey, 'Kerala Political Killings Are Symptomatic of Communist Regimes' Propensity to Use Violence as Tool of State Machinery', Firstpost, 20 January 2018, http:// www.firstpost.com/politics/kerala-political-killings-are- symptomatic-of-communist-regimes-propensity-to-use- violence-as-tool-of-state-machinery-4311755.html.

9. Based on interviews with several police officers, a section of the PFI leadership and on internal police documents.

10. 'Fazal Murder Case: Chilling Video of RSS Worker Confessing to Murdering PFI Man Out', News Minute, 9 June 2017, https://www.thenewsminute.com/article/fazal-murder-case- chilling-video-rss-worker-confessing-murdering-pfi-man- out-63420.

11. The killing of a young Congress leader, S.P. Shuhaib, who was repeatedly hacked with a machete below his waist by a four-member gang of suspected CPI(M) men in early February 2018, has turned the tide against the ruling government. The victim had forty-one stab wounds, according to the post-mortem report. But the CPI(M), which leads the government, maintains that such deaths are often preceded by clashes targeted at their party functionaries.